The V...
An Unorthodox Soldier's Memoirs

T.S. Lewis

Copyright © 2019 T.S. Lewis Publishing LLC

All rights reserved. No part of this book may be reproduced in any form by any electronic or mechanical means without the expressed written permission of the author, except by a reviewer, who may quote brief passages in a review.

ts.lewis.publishing@outlook.com

ISBN: 9781791384425

DEDICATION

For those who didn't make it home.
"No day shall erase you from the memory of time."
—*Virgil*

A portion of the proceeds will be donated to an organization that helps veterans.

TABLE OF CONTENTS

	Acknowledgments	5
	Acronyms	6
1	Barely Audible	7
2	Garryowen	20
3	September 11	30
4	Combat Patch	40
5	Vilseck	52
6	Baghdad	69
7	Area of Operations	85
8	Missing Home	101
9	Learning Curves	113
10	Tactical Operations Center	132
11	Digitized Warfare	144
12	Baqubah	158
13	Reintegration	169

ACKNOWLEDGMENTS

Thanks to Y. Loden, Jackie Jackson, E. Bell, N. Simon, C. Stately, C. Bennett, Mat (XO) Bocian, K. Wing, S. Seikaly, L. Harris, Iris Rafi, H. Shepherd, Dr. Ned Loader, and WriteByNight LLC for helping me become better. I would be remiss if I didn't extend a special thanks to the Fort Bliss Mental Health and Speech Pathology departments.

I hoped to use the names of fallen heroes I collected from the *Stars and Stripes* newspaper for the book cover. Out of respect for the families and copyright infringement, I used some headlines instead. I honor those who gave more than me.

To family, friends, and fans, your support and encouragement has been immeasurable.

The color of humanity is love with shades of struggle. Thank you for coloring my struggles with love.

ACRONYMS

AO – Area of Operations
BFV – Bradley Fighting Vehicle
COP – Command Outpost
CASH – Combat Aid Station Hospital
ECP – Entry Control Point
EFP – Explosively Formed Penetrator
FOB – Forward Operating Base
IED – Improvised Explosive Device
IBA – Interceptor Body Armor
KIA – Killed in Action
LT – Lieutenant
LNO – Liaison Officer
MEDEVAC – Medical Evacuation
MOS – Military Occupational Specialty
NCO – Noncommissioned Officer
NCOER – (NCO) Evaluation Report
OP – Observation Post
QRF – Quick Reactionary Force
RPG – Rocket Propelled Grenade
ROTC – Reserve Officer Training Corps
S-2 – Intel Section
TOC – Tactical Operations Center
USO – United Services Organization
UAV – Unmanned Aerial Vehicle

Military time runs 24 hours. Therefore, 0 or 2400 = midnight. 0100 = 1st hour; 1200 = noon; 1300 = 13th hour, all the way to midnight.

BARELY AUDIBLE

El Paso sunset

"Most of the important things in the world have been accomplished by people who have kept on trying when there seemed to be no hope at all." —Dale Carnegie

For the first time in 40-plus years of living, I came to the conclusion that writing was overrated and when this story unexpectedly vanished from the computer screen, I wanted to smash every piece of electronic equipment I owned with a ball peen hammer. That's how I felt three pages into authorship.

Usually, I rose from bed performing my preliminary routine: brushing my teeth, peeing, then letting a Shih Tzu named Flex outside to relieve himself. This time he sniffed the patio's three vacant corners and raised his leg at the fourth where a bag of charcoal leaned against a rusted grill. It was brisk, unusual weather for El Paso in late autumn. The wind reached its tentacles around the door as I forced it shut upon Flex's reentry.

The next step in that routine involved emptying the dishwasher then making a bowl of cinnamon raisin oatmeal. That routine changed when I plonked in front of a ten-year-old laptop and began the painstaking task of typing a story when I didn't even recognize the hero I once was.

A week prior, I had been prescribed a heart monitor. It was a bulky device that stuffed in a pocket with three sticky electrodes that attached to my torso. When the patches stayed on longer than a day, it produced an irritating rash. Therefore, the nodes needed to be offset from one spot to the next. The device was to be worn for two weeks excluding showers.

The reason for the device prompted me to write this story. I suffered a cerebral infarction on November 12, 2015. The device monitored my heart to ascertain where the blood clot originated.

Although I had taken some creative writing classes and written prose and poems, I never imagined I'd publish a book. Having had a stroke, I found the necessary motivation to stop wishing and start doing.

A month prior, my wife, Tia, survived a motorcycle accident that I witnessed. After her accident and my inability to effectively talk, the realization of a medical retirement weighed on me. Life had thrown a powerful one-two punch at us.

My anxiety carried me nine months into the future when I would end twenty-two years of military service. I hadn't planned on being medically discharged. What would I do?

Being unable to speak was sobering. U.S. cavalrymen didn't have ischemic strokes. We were the guys with sabers drawn, hootin' and yellin' "Charge," riding on horseback into a fray of cannon fire. The stroke was full blown and life-threatening. My youth vanished. Notions of superhuman powers evaporated, and a dark cloud materialized overhead. Each drop that ensued weighed ten pounds and slapped me deeper into the ground.

It occurred around 0530 hours (5:30 a.m.). I was performing morning preliminaries when I felt disoriented. Tia chatted from our small bathroom about her job and the administrative difficulties she was having with army doctors wrapping their big-picture minds around minuscule office details. As she hummed along, I responded with the usual male responses, "uh-uh" and "hmm-hmm," from our bedroom, then silence.

I felt deathly ill as if my brain had plunged into my stomach and its acid was causing a psychedelic trip. Was this the biblical death for past sins I read about?

I lay on the side of the bed where my wife could not witness my transition. She finished brushing rouge on her cheeks and stood by the door, still chatting to herself. After sixty-five seconds of fatalistic thinking, heat rushed through my veins. I needed to FIGHT! *Get up!* My inner voice shouted. *It's not time to die!* My mind pushed buttons trying to retract my soul from departure.

I sprang up with machine-like efficiency, and she became concerned when her questions went unanswered. I attempted to turn off the TV, but the button kept dodging my thumb. Frustrated, I threw the remote on the bed.

"Lewis? Lewis! Look at me," Tia said.

My gaze focused on the closet behind her. I could barely utter, "yeah." She asked several questions. In my mind, I answered them with full sentences, but all that came out was, "yeah."

"Can you hear me?" she asked.

"Yeah" was barely audible. In my mind I yelled, *I'm dying*, as I dueled against my tongue. I lost control of volume—my brain was shutting off.

"What's wrong with you?" she pleaded. "I think you're having a stroke!"

Finally, she named the life or death game of charades as the right side of my face drooped. Her quick reaction saved my life. I was rushed to University Medical Center (UMC), where they have one of the best neurological teams in the country. The paramedics were exceptional too. Instead of taking me to the army hospital, where they didn't have recombinant tissue plasminogen activator treatment, they rushed me to UMC.

In that situation, minutes made the difference between permanent disability or death and being able to dress oneself or swallow food. Initially, speaking was the least of my worries. I fought the right side of my body to maintain mobility. Ironically, being a man of few words, I desperately wanted to speak. Had I known how close I was to paralysis; I might have been more concerned about that instead of answering Tia.

Once the medicine entered my system, roughly an hour and a half later, I was able to uncurl my right fist and wiggle my fingers. It was still a struggle to speak, but a loud "NO" returned to my vocabulary. I cried profusely when Tia and our sons came into the intensive care room. I had prepared to die mentally and was reawakened to how life could be. That day, I thwarted death.

As the day progressed and people visited, I was able to scribble a few words so they could comprehend my garbled speech. What a joy it was to write. Scribbles on a notepad became symbolic. It made me hopeful for the recovery that lay ahead. The two-week device was upgraded to an implant. It would be months before it recorded the odd flutters of my heart.

In preparation for my medical retirement, I had taken the Myers-Briggs' personality test. According to it, writer topped the list. I am an introvert and loner by nature. A supervisor once described me by telling our boss, "He's a scout. He goes out alone with a small contingent and hides in the woods. Not even the squirrels know he's there. Why in the world would he come greet you?"

So, the personality test seemed rational, but the idea of arranging words and sentences together so that people spent money to read them didn't seem plausible.

The supervisor who had described my level of introversion was a retired lieutenant colonel who was well-versed in special operations. He summed up my previous job description well. He explained what it meant to be a scout to a lieutenant colonel reservist who had an issue when I only saluted and said, "Good morning, sir," per army regulations.

For whatever reason, he needed more sunshine in my disposition. That wasn't me. I was horrible at stroking egos. Myers-Briggs' second choice was sanitation engineer. I would be satisfied cleaning toilets at a local high school. At least I wouldn't have to shake anyone's hand.

Most of my army superiors didn't care for my demeanor. I was called unorthodox on more than one occasion, not a team player on a few, and I am sure other labels were affixed to me of which I was unaware. I didn't care about the politics supervisors played. Nine out of ten soldiers that I led would probably have a beer with me. Trainees from basic training would probably hold me in the highest regard, just as I held my drill sergeants in the highest esteem.

So it was, and is, with many in the army. Ninety-nine percent of us have a love-hate relationship with good leaders because they made us clean up our lives. They did not accept us until they had the best of us. Mediocre was never an option. Fail miserably or succeed exceedingly. Halfway meant you were boondoggling.

Before I get too far along, my name is Ted Lewis, retired U.S. Army sergeant first class with twenty-two years of service, husband, and father of three. Deuce is the eldest. He bent and rearranged rules to his liking. Diamond, my only girl, is a one-woman dance ensemble, tall with magazine- cover beauty. My youngest, Ryan, is a timid introvert. He stays in the core center of himself and stays in his room so much, I think he draws cave paintings to communicate to the future world. Of course, there is Tia, my lovely wife who passed her cover-girl beauty to our daughter.

As for me, I love America, yet hated going to Iraq. My ethnicity—soiled, the way we all are. Religion—I believe in something, but don't know what it is after deploying to Iraq. Went from Pentecostal to nondenominational. I used to capitalize God—now I can write "god" without fear of being sent to hell. Hard to believe in an all-powerful being when man has categorized Him based on geography. Where we're born determines the kind of heaven we'll enter is a limited way of thinking.

Common sense has somewhat freed most of my Sundays. I stopped believing in hell, so I've been able to forgo church altogether and sleep in on Sundays. I stopped giving credence to religion; however, I remain spiritually inquisitive about my inward journey. Anyway, as stated, I'm horrible with hello.

A Facebook post from my former high school Japanese teacher also prompted me to sit on an uncomfortable wooden chair, using an outdated laptop whose "c" key registered sporadically. He wrote: I have been waiting for you to stop ignoring who you are.

It read like a fortune cookie, but I found it profound because it aligned with the personality test. In high school, I had written a farewell essay for my teachers, thanking them for the tools they provided. I am sure that essay, plus other insights I had written through the years, stoked his encouragement.

When I began having nightmares about having another stroke and replaying my wife's accident, I sought professional help. Counseling helped push this story into existence. Most of it was written during a 15-month deployment to Iraq in 2007. The actual journal collected dust in my garage. In December 2015, a psychiatrist listened to my ordeal and immediately diagnosed me with post-traumatic stress disorder (PTSD).

"No way! Not me. There's guys who went through some rough stuff in Iraq," was my response. It wasn't until a Social Security examiner confirmed PTSD that I acknowledged the diagnosis. Scouts were hard-headed creatures. The PTSD diagnosis was added as a condition for my medical retirement, which extended my time on active duty by several months. That additional time allowed me to save more money before moving east to be near family.

Once I accepted that I had PTSD, I pulled the journal off a garage shelf. Stuffed among the journal's pages were articles, snippets that captured heroic acts of warriors who would never return home. I had written poems and prose, rants and prayers about fear of dying in Iraq and goals to accomplish upon returning home. A few entries were scribbled on napkins while walking from the dining hall. Family pictures were taped to the inside. My son Ryan posed in a batter's stance wearing his Vilseck red-and-white baseball uniform. My wife wore my taupe blazer, her legs proactively spread but hidden by the back of a chair. A few reminders of the good ole red, white, and blue that went with me during my deployment.

During the deployment, I thought journaling would be a productive way to mark time. I wasn't ready to open the journal, but life pushed me toward it. The stroke showed life was too short to leave things shelved.

The journal was an oversized green army supply books that supply techs used to track items for accountability. The journal was mostly forgotten until that point, some seven years after Iraq. I blew on its cover as sunlight from a window pierced the dust cloud that floated upwards. A musky odor escaped upon opening it. I sneezed. A brownish mite with its legs moving a million millimeters per second scurried toward the shade of the journal's center. No doubt it had been snacking on the microscopic fibers that jutted from its pages. As if protecting the journal from an unwanted invader, I smeared its insides in a streak of oblivion with my finger. That was that, an all too familiar ending to a new beginning.

Even though the sun shined in Iraq constantly, it was a haunting place. It was time to trade darkness for light. Even if it was a millisecond of illumination, that flash of hope might orient someone else in a better direction.

After typing the first paragraph, feelings of inferiority stabbed at me from the screen. Who was I to tell this story? My platoon was a sector removed from the horrific scenes that unfolded across the river. Would anyone want to read this? Would the words feel right coming from someone who identified as a janitor rather than a writer? Most importantly, would I be able to honor warriors who were more heroic than I could ever be?

PTSD feels like continually being on guard. Whenever I went to sleep, my unconscious mind would take over. I defended my body from an unseen devil with a thick index finger ready to smear me into oblivion. Tia said I constantly jumped and fought in my sleep, frequently waking in cold sweats.

My buddies saw more carnage than I did. They didn't guard against the devil's finger. They most likely welcomed him in to play cards during the witching hour. As I ran from the finger, they never bothered seeking cover. They wanted to win back souls the devil had claimed.

My platoon wasn't entering houses rigged to kill, or if we did, God intervened on our behalf. Although we were lucky, I lived vicariously through buddies who had entered those deathtraps. I saw terror replayed on the screens of their darkened pupils. They never had to say what happened. Silence painted that picture.

I remember one particular incident when I worked in the tactical operations center (TOC) and had to coordinate an air medical evacuation (MEDEVAC) after an attack that involved a house-borne explosion. It was a tense moment.

Once the platoon returned to base, I sat with Specialist Burkhart on the back steps of the TOC while he awaited instructions from our sergeant major. We hung out a few times at barbecues and played in some pick-up basketball games before we deployed. Burkhart was my choice whenever it was my pick. He exuded a warrior's mentality.

Transfixed on the TOC steps, he appeared to be stuck on hell's threshold, wanting to step into or away from that abyss he witnessed an hour ago. His stare fixated in a subconscious realm. Was he replaying the incident?

I wondered if Burkhart's mind took him to the beginning of the day before dust and sand had time to cake on the squad's sweaty uniform crotches and armpits. Every mission started out optimistically. Sitting there with him, I witnessed hope fade.

Burkhart had watched his noncommissioned officer (NCO) Jeremy Vrooman take charge and enter the house first. Vrooman wasn't supposed to be there. He chose to leave his wife, newborn baby and the safety of rear detachment to protect his men. It was his foot that tripped the pressure plate causing the stairwell to erupt. Chaos and confusion rained down. The sheer force of the explosion nearly separated Vrooman's soul from flesh as the stairs splintered into a million fragments perforating the team members behind him.

The scent of TNT and iron permeated everywhere. Ears rang and shouting was muffled. All the ghosts from wars past swirled around that room searching for more soldiers to consume. After the concussive force blew my buddy into the street, he gathered himself and muddled toward Staff Sergeant Vrooman and rendered first aid.

Everyone in the TOC focused on dispatching a Blackhawk to their location as Vrooman fought to stay on this side of eternity. Sitting next to me hours later, Burkhart replayed a gruesome cycle of entering, exploding, and repeating. Perhaps, he would drift back toward that moment indefinitely.

I wasn't there physically, but I was emotionally. In many ways, that explosion left an emotional residue on me. For years I asked, "Why did Sergeant V have to die?" Sometimes, still do.

That's what I mean when I compared my buddies' PTSD to mine. Mine was peripheral. Theirs was birthed at hell's epicenter. The day Staff Sergeant V, a man recently promoted to fatherhood, was critically injured, was when my faith finally faltered.

When I began writing this story, I hoped it would influence America's political landscape. That it would somehow curb our need to feed the military-industrial juggernaut's appetite. I know it was a grandiose wish, but I'd be remiss if I didn't mention the 156 congressmen and twenty-three senators who voted against the Iraq invasion. Still, it saddens me knowing we should never have been there.

Now that the story has been written and has flowed to its truth, I realize it encompasses so much more than a question or a collection of memories. It serves as bullhorn so other veterans may share their stories. I am sure I wasn't the only one asking why we invaded Iraq.

Civilian readers may gain a better understanding when thanking veterans for their service. Perhaps, this story may help civilian readers know a little bit more about the war on terror and what happens when you expend bullets to erase an ideology. In many ways, the story serves as a reminder that no matter where we find ourselves, or what condition to which we have fallen, we can be better. We owe that to our fallen veterans.

Note 1: Here's a rundown of enlisted rank/pay grades: E1-3 are privates; E-4 specialists or corporals; E5 and 6 sergeants and staff sergeants; E-7 platoon sergeants or sergeants first class; E-8 first sergeants or master sergeants; and E-9 sergeants major (either operational or command).

Note 2: Units composition from smallest to largest—two teams make a squad—four squads comprise a platoon —four platoons make up a troop (company)—four to six troops make up a squadron (battalion). And four squadrons make up a regiment (brigade). And the echelons continue all the way up to the commander in chief.

These notes may help civilian readers make sense of army lingo.

GARRYOWEN

Fort Hood, Texas, was home to the City Lights nightclub and Rancier Avenue, where anything and everything intersected with circus-like flair. The central Texas base was the largest installation in the army, where three mass shootings had occurred. The first was in 1991 at a Luby's cafeteria, where a gunman killed twenty-three people. The second and third affected me personally and happened in 2009 and 2014.

Adding more circus flair to Garryowen, there was a sexual harassment and assault preventer NCO convicted for overseeing a prostitution ring in 2015. Fort Hood had always been a place where controversy and the unimaginable collided. Fort Hood provided the stage for my formative years as a leader, so it was only right to begin here.

One of the cadets I taught as a Reserve Officers' Training Corps (ROTC) instructor at Methodist University, Fayetteville, North Carolina, in 2009, was shot during the third mass shooting, in April 2014. Lieutenant John Arroyo was a Green Beret before commissioning. He alerted other soldiers that the shooter, Specialist Ivan Lopez, entered a nearby building. Lopez allegedly snapped when his chain of command revoked his leave. Consequently, he killed two and injured fourteen others before killing himself.

For his valorous actions, Arroyo received a Soldier's Medal, the highest noncombat honor available. Now he tours the country speaking about Christ and how divine intervention was with him that fateful April day.

Arroyo said during his award ceremony, "I give all the glory to God because I took a .45 to the throat and lived. But this medal isn't about me. I accept this award for the soldiers who lost their lives that day, and for the soldiers and leaders who made lifesaving decisions. Without them, my wife would be receiving this award, not me... No way was I going to lay on the ground. It is going to take a lot more than a .45 to take a Green Beret out," according to the *People* magazine website.

I told my son Deuce that John had been shot. John counseled my son a few times when I brought him to work while he was suspended from school. John was raised on L.A. streets and was able to relate to my son better than I could.

Unfortunately, my son, just shy of eighteen, experienced the deaths of several friends. One was killed playing chicken with an unaware motorist. The kid was walking in the middle of the road around midnight with cars whizzing by at sixty miles per hour. I assumed he was dressed in dark clothes. Neither the accident scene nor the boy's death scared young people to live more cautiously.

Two other friends were shot within months of that incident, one fatally. The other was a flesh wound to the buttocks, which meant he was running away from trouble, which represented progress. A few years later, Deuce's best friend jumped to his death from a bridge, so

John being shot didn't faze him. He was accustomed to life abusing exclamation points.

The 2014 shooting left me stuck solving life's pauses and comma splices. To me, the 2014 mass shooting was like shooting a gun to apply periods throughout this paragraph. It was overkill. My son and his friends had already adapted to the world as a troubled place. I hoped for fairytale endings.

While researching the latest shooting, I came across the 2009 shooting. The second mass shooting involved an army psychiatrist named Nidal Hasan. He went on a jihadist murder spree, killing twelve and injuring thirty-one.

On the NBC News website, there was a photo of Sergeant Fanuaee Vea dressed in black pants and a gray physical training shirt turned inside out. His Duke Nukem-style haircut recently fashioned. His tattooed Samoan arm was draped around Private Savannah Green, whom I did not know.

Vea had always been protective and loyal. It was fitting that he was still at Fort Hood protecting someone else.

What the photo didn't reveal was the shark bite on Vea's upper thigh. He was my Bradley Fighting Vehicle (BFV) gunner in 2001. He had sustained a ten-inch bite while swimming near his native island. I asked him about it during a field training exercise in our cramped Bradley turret.

"What happened when the shark bit you?" I asked.

"I punched it," he replied, peering into his periscope, scanning our assigned hilltop for enemy.

"And then?" I dug, raising my head out of the hatch to listen for tracked vehicles moving south toward our camouflaged defensive line.

"It swam away." He switched a dial above his head to zoom in on a critical intersection at the bottom of the hill as we chuckled.

I laughed because he went back in the water once the wound stopped bleeding. He laughed because he punched a shark. *He had foolish courage,* I thought as I ducked inside to avoid the chilled night air.

When Vea and I were stationed in 1st Squadron, 7th Cavalry Regiment, aka Garryowen, we led a soldier who had been convicted of armed robbery. The unit was called Garryowen because that was General Custer's favorite Irish drinking song; therefore, the ground rules for abusing alcohol were laid in the 1800s. Our inexperienced thief robbed another soldier at an off-post ATM. Every time I visited him in the Bell County jail, he cried behind the plexiglass and pleaded his case. He denied his crime all the way up until the gavel slammed.

During his sentencing, he told the prosecution that our platoon sergeant punched him after he had been transferred into military custody. Vea allegedly witnessed that part, but conveniently developed amnesia.

I was a staff sergeant then and had my hands full taking care of knucklehead soldiers like the ATM bandit. The post commander must've felt tremendous pressure protecting us from ourselves. Fort Hood was where I learned how to juggle in the army's drunken circus.

Later in 2001, the platoon sergeant Vea had protected retired, and I took over his duties. The job felt like Daddy Daycare. Leading the lower enlisted men was easy, but getting the junior staff sergeants to follow me was a Napoleonic feat. Staff Sergeant Christie was nine years my elder and resented that I was in charge. Knowing what I know now, I would have deferred the position to him. It would have been less stressful.

Nevertheless, it was an opportunity to learn and grow. The hot seat was a great place to hone leadership skills. My first sergeant and the other senior platoon sergeants mentored me. I performed well partly because of them. The tricky part was managing middle management when I was a mid-level manager.

Because of my inability to bridge the communication gap with the staff sergeants, I often told them to get lost while the soldiers and I worked. Normally, that approach would have alienated me from the NCOs, but for whatever reason, it caused them to linger in the background, assisting whenever they saw an opportunity. We learned to function in a dysfunctional environment.

I remember one incident that involved Staff Sergeant Arnold and Sergeant Bustamante, aka Busta Rhymes because he was always beatboxing. They rented an off-post apartment together. Because they were both in the same section, I advised against it. Within a month, Arnold relinquished his authority. Bustamante showed up late and failed to accomplish tasks. I recommended that Arnold counsel Busta Rhymes. He was hesitant, so I counseled Busta.

The following day, Arnold came to work incredulously. "What did you do?" he asked.

"I gave him a 4856" (a counseling form).

After that, Arnold became an English professor. He counseled soldiers good, bad, and indifferent. Even had Busta writing counseling statements. Once infractions went on paper, soldiers felt the water getting hot. Meaning they knew they were about to get roasted from a legal standpoint. Eventually, Busta and Arnold acquired separate living quarters, and middle managers added a new tool (counseling) to our toolkit.

Some years later, after the Iraq war began, Arnold was on the cover of *Army Times*. He had deployed to Iraq while I was selected for drill sergeant duty. He served as a platoon sergeant during Iraq's first democratic election and gleamed jubilantly amongst cheering Iraqis whose indigo index fingers showed that they had voted. Arnold was thrilled to be a part of history. He had celebrity appeal and was the first person I knew with an iPhone. He was always giving updates about Britney Spears or Justin Timberlake before tweets became popular. He was destined to make a newspaper cover.

I improved at leading middle managers—even the disgruntled elder. An influx of new recruits filtered in to support the war effort. NCOs who couldn't get promoted in their current occupation had an opportunity to reclassify as 19 Deltas (cavalry scouts). I gained two seasoned sergeants. One was a mechanic: proficient in maintenance; not so much in tactics. The other was a Patriot missile operator: proficient in fieldcraft; not so much in administrative tasks.

The mechanic spearheaded our maintenance program. Unfortunately, wars in Afghanistan and Iraq limited training time to hone NCO-level scout skills. Training was geared toward urban warfare, clearing buildings, establishing traffic control points, and detecting improvised explosive devices (IEDs). Doctrinal scout training such as area, route (road) and zone reconnaissance, and in-depth screens were temporarily shelved. Therefore, the mechanic was at a disadvantage compared to his peers as it pertained to maneuvering.

As I look back, I should have coached him with sand table drills (practice running section maneuvers on terrain models) until sand spilled from our ears. During that time, training him would have shifted my focus off easy targets to 300-meter moving targets. I struggled to hit fifty-meter targets and juggled to keep soldiers from going to jail. I didn't have the leadership skill set to get him up to speed.

Typically, he would have gained that knowledge through career progression and education, but because of his combat support background, he missed learning it. Plus, the war in Afghanistan was doctrinally terrain driven, whereas Iraq was a counterinsurgency with systems and procedures still in development. Hence, I evaluated him from a doctrinal standpoint.

When his evaluation was due, he received excellent marks for administration, physical fitness, and leadership, yet needed improvement tactically. He couldn't navigate from one tree to the next. He disagreed with my assessment, but I had the counseling to justify it. What I did not have was the wherewithal to properly train and mentor him. I was trapped in big-picture thinking. The whole army was.

Case in point: in 2003, Jessica Lynch's unit was supposed to drive around a town near Nasiriyah, Iraq, but due to a navigational error, convoyed through it. That mishap led to an ambush which got eleven soldiers killed in action (KIA). Her unit's weaknesses were exploited. During the ambush, Jessica tried to return fire, but couldn't perform a primary task to unjam her rifle. One failure after another. She was later rescued and hailed as a hero. She said she wasn't a hero, but a survivor.

If that incident had not occurred, the army might not have awakened from its technological superiority complex. We entered the combat arena with substandard equipment. Jessica's unit wasn't the only example of the army falling into a Rip Van Winkle sleep. A news reporter ran a story about soldiers who dug through scrap metal heaps to harden their vehicles against IEDs. Most of the vehicles had flimsy protection. Sometimes nothing more than vinyl—kitchen flooring provided better protection.

Secretary of Defense Donald Rumsfeld had said, "You go to war with the army you have, not the army you want."

Was I using that same mindset with the mechanic? Was I using his strengths while ignoring his weaknesses, hoping the bluff worked? Couldn't we properly equip ourselves before toppling a regime?

Bush's administration lied to the American people to subsidize government contracts at the behest of Vice President Dick Cheney. If the administration lied, the army followed suit. It sold the mechanic and the field-savvy NCO on a theoretical notion that changing jobs would get them promoted, but that was dependent on some essential criteria: fundamental knowledge.

Luckily, I learned what not to do from Lynch's unit. I may not have known how to fix the mechanic's deficiency, but I knew enough to write his evaluation accordingly. Many leaders would have written that he was good when he wasn't.

Opposite of the mechanic, the Patriot missile operator wasn't worth a paperweight in garrison, but was an avid marksman and proficient in a field environment. He earned a Soldier's Medal while driving home one night on Highway 190. He witnessed a woman being set on fire. The woman's boyfriend doused her with kerosene and tossed a lit cigarette in her direction. The Patriot operator, a short, scrappy, Jed Clampett-looking fellow, sprang into action. He called 911 and smothered her flames. Sadly, she went back to her abuser months later and died from an overdose, if I recall correctly.

Similar to the mechanic, he believed that reclassing was the correct path for promotion, even though they both neared twenty years of federal service. Had they transitioned earlier; they would have had a few years to acquire that experience. The Department of Defense dangled a proverbial carrot of promotion over less combat-oriented military occupational specialties (MOS) to beef up combat MOSs.

Subsequently, the army implemented a "quantity over quality" recruitment strategy. No diplomas were necessary. Criminals with misdemeanors were accepted with no questions asked. Lesser felonies slipped through loopholes. It didn't matter as recruiters figured out ways to increase manpower. As numbers increased, discipline decreased.

Everyone deserved a second, and sometimes a third or fourth chance, but the army wasn't offering second chances, not really. When they needed us, they needed us. When they didn't, they downsized as they had done after Desert Storm (1991). The mechanic and the Patriot operator were no exceptions, and September 11 would soon be upon us.

Terrorists would shout "Allahu Akbar" as they gained access to the cockpits of American Airlines flights 11 and 77 and United Airline flights 175 and 93. "Allahu Akbar" would lock god in a phrase of hate.

Allahu Akbar, God is Great, probably the last phrase the four flights heard. Why did He let "Allah" slip through the insurgents' lips? Maybe God didn't want to shut them up? Perhaps it was His way to bring the victims solace amid destruction?

The war on terror would soon be convoluted with confusion. I hoped "Allahu Akbar" would not strike fear or ignite visions of horror. Radicals chose a phrase that preyed upon our religious differences. As long as we associated a godly phrase with destruction, we would always be divided.

That fear and intolerance would perpetuate the storm that lay ahead. We were about to experience the tipping point of hate. God is great was about to widen our divide and have us in a continual reactive state.

SEPTEMBER 11

"Those who love peace must learn to organize as effectively as those who love war." —Martin Luther King Jr.

Fort Hood was destined to alter my life. For the next hundred years, September 11 would be, for those of us who witnessed it unfold on television, the most poignant moment of our lives. Alzheimer's could not erase it from our collective memory.

On September 11, 2001, 7th Cavalry was three and a half weeks into a month-long field training exercise. For those who may not know, the 7th Cavalry fought in the Battle of Little Bighorn commanded by General Custer. It was also commanded by Colonel Hal Moore during the Vietnam War. He coauthored *We Were Soldiers Once... and Young*.

Having been raised in church, I was still religious at the turn of the millennium, so I had Vea stencil II Chronicles 32:7-8 on our Bradley Fighting Vehicle's tube-launched, optically tracked (TOW) missile launcher. The King James version read: "Be strong and courageous. Do not be afraid or discouraged because of the king of Assyria and the vast Army with him, for there is a greater power with us than with him. With him is only the arm of flesh, but with us is the LORD our God to help us fight our battles."

Other crews in the troop stenciled slogans such as Colossus, Collateral Damage, and Cold Steel on their M1A3 (Abrams) tank gun tubes or TOWs. In total, there were nine tanks and thirteen BFVs in Comanche Troop. Each troop within the squadron—Apache, Bandit, and Delta—named their war chariots with an A, B, or D name. For example, Assassin and Aftermath, or Braveheart or Dare Devil. It took creative flair to come up with catchy phrases that added to each crew's individuality. None was more unique than ours.

We were a different crew. We didn't cuss, smoke, or chew tobacco. Well, I didn't cuss until the day Veloz, our squinty-eyed driver, blazed a trail across a training area and sent twenty-five tons of spaced laminate armor airborne. He couldn't see a minor wadi that lay ahead.

"Veloz, slow down!" I screamed. The scream probably shorted out the intercom's effectiveness.

He proceeded with full momentum into the dry creek embankment, ramming Vea's face into his periscope and crushing my hip into the cheaply padded hatch. The impact sent dirt airborne. The laws of physics were the only reasons the vehicle slowed. Veloz said, "My bad sarge," and kept charging toward the high ground as I cussed him up one side and down the other. Up until that point, we were cherries.

A few old-timers had served in Desert Storm. Many of them neared retirement. A few deployed to Bosnia. Some to Somalia. Half of us anticipated punching our combat ticket. As a matter of fact, Corporal Peterson worked as our training room NCO. He was a helicopter door gunner in Somalia and fired countless rounds protecting soldiers who had been pinned below.

For him, Somalia was personal, because he knew the soldier who had been immortalized in the movie *Blackhawk Down*. His body had been dragged through Mogadishu's streets. It was his story that inspired the scripture on my BFV. I wanted God close by in case we were ever sent into combat.

On September 11, unbeknownst to us, the second plane erupted against the second tower while we were in the middle of a twenty-kilometer zone reconnaissance. Our fighting vehicles were arrayed linearly with 100 meters between in each vehicle. We inched down dirt trails so our tracks didn't produce a dust signature. The tanks crept behind us, waiting for our alert to bring them forward to kill whatever enemy our 25-millimeter main gun couldn't destroy.

We checked streams, creeks, ponds, anthills, dirt trails improved or unimproved, and grassy knolls to confirm or deny enemy presence. While verifying my position on the map, Comanche Six's (our commander) voice crackled in our headsets, I pressed the helmet closer to my ears so I could hear over the Bradley's diesel engine. "Cease all training. Break. Meet me at grid coordinates: Papa Victor two-zero-fife-fower-fower-ait in wun-fife mikes-over (PV 205448 in 15 minutes)," he said.

Staff Sergeant Arnold was the only person I knew with an iPhone with an unlimited data plan. I was still on a free plan after 1900 hours (7 p.m.). Arnold provided more detail by saying, "America is under attack." Though no one knew what that meant, we knew it was fresh and happening.

We had two historical reference points: Pearl Harbor and the Oklahoma City bombing. Even as the sun reached its apex, we were left in utter darkness. Sometimes not knowing something was better than knowing it. Vea and Veloz batted ideas back and forth. Maybe this? Maybe that? Our imagination was in the stone age compared to the reality of what we were about to discover.

The troop congregated around Comanche Six at the bottom of a hill that dominated the area. Veloz was briefed to always park under a tree whenever possible. He drove with his hatch closed while the sun attacked Vea and me in the turret. He found our clock position within the tactical perimeter and tucked our Bradley underneath a tree—weapon systems pointing outward protecting Comanche Six's tank in the center.

Once everyone shut their engines off and dismounted toward the center, our leader said, crestfallenly, "Go home and spend time with your families." He seemed to know more but couldn't articulate what he wanted to say.

I had never experienced training ending early or a leader who was rendered speechless. This was serious. Had we been nuked? Fear made my skin tingle as if the rapture had taken place and my unit was the only one left behind. Looking back, that or an atomic bomb would have been better than what I was about to learn.

The usual ten-minute drive home took three and a half hours. I was glad to know the rapture had left more than just my unit behind. I didn't recall if the radio made mention of the details other than that New York had been hit. I arrived at my modular home around 1500 hours (3 p.m.). I remember standing in my carpeted living room with muddied boots. The remote control was in my hand as I listened to a news commentator hold back sobs. My mouth gaped open as Flight 11 slammed into the North Tower. *Holy Mother of all things unnatural!*

All the missing ideas formulated in the field gave way to sheer lunacy. *Where was the mushroom cloud? This couldn't be real.* When a second plane veered into the South Tower, an orange plume ballooned and disappeared. The television became an abyss that sucked me into utter disbelief. I was paralyzed. I became distinctly aware that war was being birthed. Not that I wanted war, but I knew this required retaliation.

Gravity loosened its pull, the walls at 3034 Canterbury Drive disintegrated, and the roof hovered overhead. The network replayed the footage. When the first plane disintegrated this time, the remote slipped from my grasp, my knees buckled, and downward I went. Everything fell in unison: remote, knees, and towers. People scattered from the debris cloud. The walls reappeared. Our family pictures hanging on the wall sharpened into focus as if the camera that had initially taken the photographs had been out of focus. I remained on my knees with my hands folded in prayer. I understood what Arnold meant by "America is under attack."

Escapees of the debris cloud were disoriented. Their foreheads dripped with blood. Their clothes matted in building particulates. I felt New York's anguish as a man leapt to his death from 106 stories. His only choices: a slow death by fire, or let gravity and ground do it more efficiently. *Jesus Christ! Where was the rapture?* An hour must have passed before reality retracted from that unnatural state of disbelief.

Before 9/11, I described myself as religious. I participated in the Unseen Hands Ministry at church. We cleaned the church after service. I was a good servant serving God the best way I knew. I reached my monthly tithe quota and gave more by supplying janitorial services for free. I should have valued my time more. I never thought of time as a commodity. Everyone seemed to put their affairs in order after September 11, but I soldiered on as if time was infinite. The months after 9/11 were the toughest time of my life, up to that point.

I remember asking God why my wife had grown distant when we were so involved in church. When God didn't answer, I asked her. She didn't want to answer, so I confronted her with hotel receipts. With tears streaming down our faces, she mentioned how I neglected her after 9/11. She needed consoling and I acted nonchalantly. She was afraid I was going off to war. She needed reassurance that life would be fine after such a horrific ordeal. She needed a comforter instead of the rigidity of knight's armor.

Before my confrontation, I reflected how our relationship had changed over the past several months. How our sleeping habits changed. How she became absent while being there. How space invaded our closeness. When I held her at night, I could feel air between us. I had never felt that before. We used to sleep skin against skin. Our faith in one another crumbled like the twin towers. We walked in the wake of rubble. I felt as if the church was a foreign entity. That somehow God turned alien and allowed distance to become commonplace.

    I didn't find out until years later the extent of her why. It's easy to understand how something occurred. It takes a little more understanding for why. Sometimes it was better to remain clueless than to venture into those intricacies. It reminded me of a scene from *Titanic*, when Rose described a woman's heart was like an ocean. That was me as a husband—riding along Tia's heart's surface not knowing the pain she hid beneath.

    We were driving to Fort Benning, Georgia, to visit an old army buddy when she revealed a painful secret she had kept since college. We often circled back to the hurt we caused each other and tried to figure out the root causes of the struggles we endured. I listened as her voice quivered against her truth. She needed me emotionally during 9/11, and I was out of tune. She carried abandonment issues and felt unwanted. She bore the burden of lust with little love in return.

    We entered into our relationship blinded by a lack of knowledge and maturity. Once the light flickered on, we weren't scared off by the ruin. We were bound by our brokenness. I placed my hand on her thigh.

    "I love you Tia," I whispered. She placed her hand on mine as the mile markers counted down. That was the closest we had been since 9/11. God had not become alien; I had.

Eventually, life readjusted. My unit was tasked with base security in the months following September 11. At first, the days on gate guard were edgy. We anticipated nefarious agents attempting to smuggle fertilizer bombs onto post, which quickly morphed into monotony. We would be euphoric whenever there was a Ford, Mazda, Toyota, and Dodge lined up to enter instead of five Fords in a row. Security duty was impactful because it laid the foundation for traffic control point operations while deployed.

Months after 9/11, security companies sprang up. Civilians replaced soldiers so that we could begin training again. The arrival of security companies was the first hint that war was a lucrative investment. The 3rd Infantry, from Fort Stewart, Georgia, deployed to Afghanistan and was the first to kick in Taliban teeth as 2002 transitioned into summer.

I hadn't meshed with the new platoon leader who arrived from West Point. He welcomed me by saying, "You're good, but I need a sergeant first class as my platoon sergeant." Not the best approach when you want to make someone feel welcome. But the West Pointer was right; he'd be better served with a more experienced NCO. I received orders for Drill Sergeant School, and his wish was granted.

When I returned from Drill Sergeant School, my first sergeant said, "It's about time you put something on your uniform," slapping my chest so the pinned-on Drill Sergeant badge left a mark.

Some people identified themselves with the badges: Air Assault, Airborne, Ranger, Pathfinder, Special Forces, etc. None were more illustrious than a combat badge. I was content being a patchless scout.

His comment reminded me of the first time I went home for Christmas during basic training wearing my army service uniform. I couldn't wait to show off my bedazzlements. That particular Sunday, another soldier returned home as well. His uniform was decked out with eye-catching Airborne wings, maroon beret, jump boots polished to a reflection, and Pathfinder tab to match.

All I had was a pathetic olive-colored cunt-cap and an Army National Defense Service ribbon. My friend Abigail was sitting next to me when the Pathfinder was ushered to his seat. She observed him. Glanced at me. Looked back at him, then stared at my uniform. "You're missing a few things, aren't you?"

"He's Airborne and falls out of perfectly good planes," I replied. We laughed quietly, as if our grandmothers were sitting nearby ready to pinch us for acting unchurchly.

Deng Ming-Dao said it best: "Some warriors look fierce but are mild. Some seem timid but are vicious. Look beyond appearances; position yourself for the advantage."

On New Year's Day 2003, we made final preparations to move to Fort Knox, Kentucky. Bush's administration had effectively sold America on weapons of mass destruction (WMDs). Regrettably, valuable assets were diverted from the Afghan fight to Iraq. If Sun Tzu were alive, he would have written a chapter called Military Blunder. He had written something to that affect when he wrote: "If it [fighting on two fronts] can be avoided, never fight a two-pronged attack." The war in Iraq became the second prong; Afghanistan was the first.

As my family headed to Fort Knox, Pandora's box widened. Iraq went from being a few months old to a couple of years old. The focus shifted from fighting Taliban in Afghanistan to al-Qaeda spreading throughout the region. Iraq, at least for me, symbolized Vietnam. I had yet to step a foot there and was secretly picketing against it. Whatever unresolved issues I had experienced during Garryowen's circus went with me to Fort Knox.

COMBAT PATCH

"The test of a good teacher is not how many questions he can ask his pupils that they will answer readily, but how many questions he inspires them to ask him which he finds hard to answer." —Alice Wellington Rollins

When I was a drill sergeant, I perfected the art of psychological warfare. Trainees aptly nicknamed me El Diablo. Before I broke them down in order to build them up, I recounted *Conan the Barbarian*.

"Who's seen *Conan the Barbarian*?" I asked, calling on a private who began forming the "Oh-I-know" lips.

"Explain what happened in the beginning of the movie," I demanded.

The jittery scout explained how Conan was chained to a mill grinder, constantly rotating its wheel in rain, humidity, snow, night and day. After years of circling the grinder, scrawny Conan grew into Arnold Schwarzenegger.

"What was the saying at the beginning of the movie?" I asked.

"That which doesn't kill me, makes me stronger, Drill Sergeant!"

"Shall we not commence to getting stronger?" I said with a devious grin.

They were now psychologically ready to place their bodies in situations normal people would have responded to with "Thanks, but no thanks." Every push-up was them saying hello to their new selves and farewell to their past selves. If their minds were conditioned, the job of building their bodies would be easier. They committed themselves to becoming Schwarzenegger. Pain was necessary for development. I provided the way; their will did the rest.

Tia said the army was designed to turn us into robots. But I wanted my guys to be thinkers as well as followers. I was introducing a new warrior class before General David Petraeus, the coalition commander for Iraq, had shifted his focus to winning Iraqi's hearts and minds. War required more than blind obedience.

Unlike my generation, many of those trainees joined because of 9/11. They had the same stuff as WWII vets. They wanted to kick ass. All I had to do was point them in the direction of the ass kicking. I was honored to have a chance to mold their fighting spirit. I prayed none of them would die in battle.

Later, I learned that one had. Even though God Himself couldn't have prevented a rocket propelled grenade (RPG) from ripping through a Stryker vehicle, I realized that my powers as a drill sergeant didn't extend beyond reality. Raindrops were weighted again. Training could not defy the realm of physics, metal density, or RPGs. Private First Class Cory Depew died in Mosul, Iraq, on January 4, 2005. He was 21.

I trained roughly 375 cavalry scouts over a three-year period. Few faces burn in my mind as vividly as Depew's. His smile was genuine. His skin adjusted to hormonal changes causing acne to dot his doughy face. Honestly, I can't remember much about his personality, just that his smile was contagious. Whenever I told him to do push-ups until the Earth shifted its axis and moved closer to the sun, he smiled and pushed until he started sweating profusely. "Is it close enough yet, Drill Sergeant," he'd ask with his non-erasable grin. He's in a cavalryman's paradise—Fiddler's Green. Rest in peace scout.

Ironically, I worked from the same office as my drill sergeants back in 1994. I will never forget drill sergeants Dunning and Fisher gathering us in their office before graduation and telling us, "Y'all are old enough to die for your country, you ought to be able to drink to it."

Most of us were kids. Barely men. Dunning and Fisher pulled out plastic cups and a bottle of bottom-shelf brown liquor from a desk drawer and toasted to us. Weird, how I followed the same tradition with my graduates. I didn't know if it was the toast at the end or the Conan speech at the beginning that allowed them to see beyond my Diablo façade. I had one goal: turn them into the best warriors possible. But in my heart of hearts, I never wanted any of them to actually pull a trigger. Perhaps I wished for something the world could never offer: peace.

Because of the surge (a period when Congress authorized more bodies to remedy problems that didn't require more bodies), most scouts spent a year at their respective units before deploying to a street in Iraq or a goat trail in Afghanistan. Private Depew spent six months in Second Squadron, Fourteenth Cavalry before deploying.

Guilt burdened me. I watched the news constantly, hoping I didn't see anyone I trained. I was stateside and they were being sent into a meat grinder. I was tasked to prepare them for something I had never experienced. I wanted to go with them. Maybe it was my religious beliefs that shaped that wish. Surely, no harm would befall me. I had God's scripture to protect me. Being stateside, I could pretend to be superman. The only kryptonite I warned them of was not being there for one another, because that was all that mattered in the end.

Eventually, I was promoted to E-7, which allowed me to attend a Senior Leader's Course, which was also at Fort Knox. School afforded me an opportunity to interact with soldiers who had been deployed to Iraq.

"Al-Qaeda are cowards. They hide and wait for us to convoy, then attack us with IEDs. They're too chickenshit to face us in the open," was one NCO's viewpoint.

They may have been cowards, but you cannot deny that it was an ingenious way to fight. Taken from the pages of Sun Tzu himself, a "Know your enemy" sort of thing. The first batch of battle-tested veterans deployed with a simplified mindset, and it was a direct reflection of our senior leadership at that time. We underestimated the problems we unleashed by invading Iraq.

Funny, I attended the Senior Leader's Course right about the time Abu Ghraib made the news. It involved leaked photos of U.S. personnel abusing detainees. Our mindset needed tweaking. Leaders higher in rank assumed the fight would end in six months and we'd be home gripping a frosty beer mug. I knew it was a romanticized notion birthed from hubris. It was scary when I reflected on the mindset of the time. We were fools then, and not much has changed.

During the war's early years, when an IED detonated, innocent Iraqis near the blast were mowed down in a hail of American lead. From ground level to building top, from the first building to the last, everything and everyone was adjudicated as an adversary.

When I deployed to Iraq years later, apartment buildings on Haifa Street were riddled with bullet holes. The holes resembled dots of graffiti waiting to be connected. If buildings could bleed, that street would have been stained scarlet. Although I had yet to deploy, I knew enough history to know enemies must be respected, or at least studied. After all, they battled the most powerful nation on Earth, and exploited our weaknesses with ancient military wisdom. No matter how senseless their ideology was, there was a vast amount of cunning involved.

Drill sergeant duty became a blessing and a curse. I was directed by the army to complete two years of duty and then involuntarily extended an additional year. From 2003 to 2006, I remained in the United States, which meant I missed a great deal of Iraq's bloodiest time. I'm amazed Depew was the only trainee that died.

Drill instructor duty may not have been as terrible as combat, but it was still taxing. During my first cycle, I saw two privates walking back to the barracks after evening chow. Privates were supposed to run everywhere. Every minute was a physical training opportunity. I corrected their behavior by making them run to the barracks, which were about 100 meters away and up twenty-five steps. I told them to run back and forth from the mess hall to the barracks until I got tired.

Dinner chow was around 1800 hours (6 p.m.). It never dawned on me after passing out mail, supervising boot cleaning, and prepping the next day's tasks that those knuckleheads were still sprinting. When I drove home at 2330 hours, the traffic light by the mess hall turned red, which gave me an opportunity to glance over and see they were barely shuffling.

Without skipping a beat, I lowered the window. "Privates, get your asses to bed and don't let me catch you walking again!" I'm glad I remedied my mistake before the command sergeant major did.

I could have been reprimanded plenty of times for trainee abuse, but luck was on my side. It was small potatoes compared to what the nation asked of them.

That's why I gained their respect on day one. I knew there would be more days they hated me than loved me. I made sure their hate was directed at a standard, and not toward me. Whenever I made blunders comparable to that one, they never knew it. To them, everything that happened was necessary, no matter how unnecessary it actually was.

My most teachable moment, whereby I became the student, and the student became instructor, involved a Nigerian specialist named Adighije, pronounced Ah-de-ja-gay. At first meet, my battle buddy, Drill Sergeant Novak called him Alphabet because his New Jersey tongue induced stroke symptoms trying to annunciate each syllable. I shortened it to DJ.

As a drill sergeant, I was charged with forming a cohesive platoon. Initially, it was challenging getting different backgrounds and races to blend as one. Intuitively, I asked DJ what his name meant.

He sang his story in his native tongue and performed a historical dance. I was blown away. I felt like I was watching Alex Haley's *Roots* with Kunta Kinte's great-grandparents directing. I immediately called Novak over and told him to watch this. Novak's mouth gaped open. "Close your mouth, Battle," I said, smirking.

After hearing it, Novak gathered all the privates in one of our twelve-men bays. There was a frizzy-redhead kid from the most rural part of Oklahoma, used to raising cattle with his father. Next to him was an olive-faced kid from the Bronx who shadowboxed at every opportunity. We had a Nebraska kid whose town resembled a patchwork of green and brown tilled fields when viewed from an airplane window. There were two Mississippians, one white, the other black, who sat close in proximity, but didn't congregate the way a congregation should. Thirty men in total sat amid metal bunk beds with sheets and drab wool blankets tucked neatly, listening to Adighije's family history unfurl the way their beds never could.

His story was passed to him from a time when his ancestors used spears to hunt antelope and followed stars north. With song and dance he explained his lineage and how he came to be named. Never before, or since, have I felt such a connection between things lost and things gained.

Although his language was foreign to us, the rhythm of his cadence caused our minds to march in unison. The gyration of his hands and feet felt familiar. It caused America to slip away, and we were left wearing humanity's garb. Clothed as one. Our existence was bound to his, at least that's how I felt, and it was my third time watching his rendition. He told his story so well, I could tell that the fairer-skinned kids, including myself, wished we could take a field trip to Africa and make earthen angels as we tanned under the sun's radiance together.

Here was this 26-year-old college graduate and multiple-language speaker telling his story as all our stories were once told, around a fire and wrapped in song so it could be remembered. There was a brilliance to it. We felt honored to bear witness to something so spectacular. We crossed time and color lines. It was chilling to watch everyone's perceptions melt away. For the briefest of moments, we weren't drill sergeants, and they weren't privates. We were men, learning from DJ's display. In a time when a lot of kids didn't know their fathers, here was a man telling us his entire lineage.

We became him, and he, us. African. American. Educated. Mature. Wise. Warriors with purpose. I'm certain it was an experience none of us would forget. We didn't need color, race, or creed if we were bound by deed. DJ revealed a missing part of all our histories, a part that had gotten lost by using too many labels. He showed us who we once were. He plugged the holes of paradise lost and his rain dance flooded our souls. That day, I had gotten being a drill sergeant right.

Twenty-four months later, NCOs who had been deployed to the war began backfilling as drill sergeants. I still couldn't fathom going to Iraq. I was amazed when those NCOs said they couldn't wait to get back to a deployable unit. They'd rather be at war than deal with the hardships of drill sergeant duty. I tried to understand their point of view, but I had no frame of reference.

We devoted time and energy preparing soldiers for war. The barracks and training were our home. Our soldiers became family. It was the natural order of things. During my last year of duty, I learned how to balance the job with my real family.

The problems from Fort Hood continued to be an old scab I picked at. I had forgiven Tia for what had happened at Fort Hood, but not by deed. It seemed we had cycles where we needed to test our love by unintentionally punishing one another.

I wanted to attribute it to her nagging. She may have felt unappreciated. Tia's first review of this manuscript suggested I divulge every detail about our relationship, but this story wasn't written for that, so a summary will have to suffice.

There was a female sergeant who had been persistently pursuing me, and that sliver of "maybe the grass was greener" caused me to leave home. Of course, Tia didn't know that I was cheating. To her, I was searching for myself. Tia came by my apartment to grab some money and became suspicious when I wouldn't incriminate myself by letting her in. She bulldozed her way through. Combat training came in handy. I was able to subdue her with minimal effort.

The incident did lead to a Barney Fife moment when the deputy sheriff who resided across the street hurried over to intervene before Tia's rage caught fire again. He drew his pistol and it tumbled onto the lawn. Instead of retrieving it, he wrestled Tia to the ground. I wanted to cry at the entire situation, but I focused on the deputy's Barney Fife moment and ignored the situation altogether. There I was failing again.

The last six months of duty was when our relationship started turning toward better. The same analogy I used to push the trainees to the grinder, I had to subject myself to as well. I learned to balance work and home toward the end. I reasserted myself in church and even started working in the Unseen Hands Ministry again.

Veterans who couldn't wait to go back to war because drill sergeant duty was unbearable made me cherish my drill sergeant badge as if it were a combat patch. As bad as drill sergeant duty was, it couldn't be worse than Iraq, could it?

The curse of drill sergeant duty was leaving home at 0430 hours and returning after midnight. Our families slept when we left and slept when we returned. Their moments between sunrise and sunset were much different from ours. They were able to search for rainbows after Kentucky thunderstorms. We'd hunker down underneath oak trees until the storm passed and kept training for war.

Looking back, I could see how Iraq might have been easier. My family survived the three-year tour. Toward the end of my tour, my butterball daughter would sometimes point out a rainbow, and I was home more often to cherish it with her.

What the duty had taken away from my family, it gave back hundredfold by providing me the knowledge to become a more effective platoon sergeant. My time of waiting came to an end. I was prepared to go to war. With that preparation, this email I received from a former trainee on October 24, 2012, reminded me of the unbreakable bond soldiers and drill sergeants shared. It was good to know that some of my teachings were impactful.

Drill Sergeant Lewis,

This is Staff Sergeant Brookings, an old trainee of yours. I was in yours and Drill Sergeant Adcock's platoon in 2005. I decided to look you up due to my current status.

I am a candidate at the United States Army Drill Sergeant School and since my time here I have done nothing but reflect upon my time under your charge. In the last 7 and a half years, I have continued to serve as a Cavalry Scout in every position from Driver to Platoon Sergeant.

Last year, I had the rare and prestigious opportunity to attend and graduate the US Army Ranger School as a Scout, as well as, in the years previous, attended Warrior Leaders Course, Advanced Leaders Course, and Air Assault. I also have served multiple tours of duty overseas as a Team Leader and Section Sergeant.

The point I want to make is that it's your unwavering professionalism and leadership that made me the Scout I am today. You brought the saying "You never forget your Drill Sergeant" to a whole new level. Not a day has gone by that I don't reminisce about standing on the ready line back at the barracks with either you or Drill Sergeant Adcock doing mail call and having us rolling on our backs laughing at the stuff y'all were saying.

You were the Drill Sergeant that turned us from boys to men and, upon graduation day, Scouts. Without taking this down memory lane too much longer, I just wanted to say thank you.

I'm currently in week 7 with 3 more weeks to go before I graduate as a Drill Sergeant and report to 5-15 CAV in December.

I can only hope to be half the Drill Sergeant you were for me and the rest of the platoon.

P.S. My last cycle will have Dixie cups and cognac, LOL.

Poignant. I was honored to be a part of something great. Honored to have known no finer men. Everyday discipline, attention to detail, and teamwork were my focus for the privates in my charge. I didn't know if I had an impact on most, but it did my soul good knowing I had for a few. Some of whom would be in my platoon (2nd Squadron, 14th Cavalry, the same unit as Cory Depew) at Fort Lewis, Washington.

Second Squadron, 14th Cavalry suffered many casualties during my last year as a drill sergeant. There was an unspoken fear that went along with knowing I was about to enter the pit of hell. I didn't know what to expect. I strapped myself into America's terror roller coaster, and as my body jiggled and jumped with the coaster's ascent, I raised my hands reluctantly, and silently screamed. The guise of Superman flew away, and I wanted off this ride.

VILSECK

Neuschwanstein Castle, Bavaria, Germany

The army offered me an assignment to Fort Lewis, Washington, with 1st Brigade, 25th Infantry, which would reflag as 2nd Stryker Cavalry Regiment prior to leaving for Germany. Second Cavalry was the oldest regiment in the army and would return to its roots during the Cold War in Bavaria, Germany, at the end of 2006. Because of my failures at Fort Hood, I knew exactly how I wanted to lead a platoon.

A few household goods were loaded on top of our Ford Expedition, and we journeyed west toward Tacoma, Washington. January wasn't an ideal time to travel northwest. We took a southern route to visit family in Georgia then encountered snow after visiting Tia's mom in Colorado. The weather cleared in Idaho and we proceeded cautiously through the snowy mountain passes of Washington. The fear that came with occasionally stomping the brakes on centrifugal-producing curves didn't diminish the state's beauty or the exhilaration I felt peering into its awe-inspiring valleys. If ever one heard the call of the wild, one heard it there.

The icy Cascade mountain passes contained rivers that outlined winding roads and steep upgrades with evergreens stopping just shy of heaven's lower limit. Pine trees were so enormous it would take three sasquatches to wrap their arms around the trunks. My soul jumped out of the truck and dived into the valley floor.

A handful of soldiers from basic training were assigned to 4th Squadron, 2nd Cavalry Regiment. One was Private Ostertag. He was an eighteen-year-old New Englander with excitable eyes. His tongue was built for snappy comebacks, but because he likened himself to a Casanova, he lacked fighting skills. He got himself into situations where Jesus debated whether to intervene.

During basic training he had my undivided attention. Most of the time, it was slap-on-the-wrist offenses. He snuck food from the mess hall or got caught in a phone booth after lights out. He gave it his best college try. I admired his raccoon-like tenacity. In many ways, he, like all the other trainees, were freshmen in the army.

After I in-processed and got settled in, I received a phone call from the platoon leader, a Marlboro-smoking Wisconsinite named Steve Drexler.

"Ostertag is at the MP station," he said with weariness in his voice. He had been dealing with a lack of discipline prior to my arrival.

"What did he do now?" I asked in an octave lower than his.

Ostertag had been stopped at Fort Lewis's main gate with an underage girl. Where might a horny eighteen-year-old attempt to hide a sixteen-year-old? IN THE TRUNK OF HIS CAR! All-caps was how Augustus, our squadron commander, screamed it to our troop commander, who shouted it to Lieutenant Drexler, who cordially relayed it to me.

The lieutenant colonel wasn't the only one upset over Ostertag's decision. All of the fathers with daughters were upset that he chose to follow a serial killer's how-to manual instead of, *I don't know,* covering her with a blanket in the back seat.

Recalling how my NCOs handled me when I did something juvenile, I persuaded Captain Maykovich to handle it at his level. The maximum company-grade punishment was fourteen days restriction and extra duty, forfeiture of one week's pay, plus a reduction in rank. Behind closed doors, I explained to the commander that we should turn this to our advantage by gaining Ostertag's unwavering loyalty. Meaning, if I kept his punishment out of the colonel's hands, Ostertag would owe the troop big time.

The Jedi mind trick worked. Ostertag served his punishment. Our commander didn't relinquish his authority. The lieutenant colonel lived to extinguish more fires started by other juveniles. And Drexler got to see his new platoon sergeant at work. Ostertag made only minor blips on the radar after that.

Drexler welcomed me with open arms, and we hit it off at first handshake. He could tap dance his way out of wet paper bag, so I didn't mind him speaking to the commander when I wasn't around. Drexler had more than just college smarts. His willingness to try different approaches while leaning on my experience was a multiplier.

There were two staff sergeants who deployed with the platoon that developed a buddy-buddy relationship with the soldiers. I told the first sergeant we didn't need them. First sergeant wasn't big on particulars. He wore a typical buzz cut and avoided failing the army's height and weight standards by having an enormously large neck that was proportional to his waistline. The two sergeants were transferred a few days later.

I was building a solid foundation and didn't want distractions. After getting rid of the two NCOs, I focused on fixing paperwork and tracking systems, and streamlined our counseling procedures. One of the things that could burn a lieutenant's career was a lack of accountability; hence, whenever we inventoried our equipment, I mimicked procedures my NCOs enforced during the mid-1990s.

Layouts were meticulous. Everything was dress-right-dress, cleaned if dirty and tagged if damaged. First Platoon (Red), Outlaw Troop was the only platoon in the squadron burning late-night oil. At 2030 hours, when the motor pool was empty, we ended our day. I told Drexler if we set the conditions right, our arrival in Germany would be smooth sailing.

Other platoons adhered to "big boy rules," a phrase they unwittingly adopted during their first deployment. As an example, we zeroed our iron sights along with the optics (magnified sights) attached to our weapons.

"But Sarge, we don't do that here. We only use optics," they griped.

"What happens when the battery dies or your optics are damaged"?

Changing culture wasn't easy. I used Jessica Lynch's leadership as a lynchpin. Eventually, we shined like polished brass. We even led the squadron in Soldier of the Month winners. Soldier of the Month boards consisted of a panel of first sergeants and the command sergeant major quizzing sergeants and lesser grades on army regulations and installation services, weapons, physical training, and leadership, among other subjects.

The reason I wanted them to go was to prepare them for the promotion board. I wanted them to score as high as possible. Plus, the first sergeants would know who they were when the time really mattered. My plan paid off. A few of my up-and-coming soldiers aced their promotion boards. I couldn't have cared less if they actually won Soldier of the Month. The fact that they did win was a testament to the NCOs preparing them. Much of the credit belonged to my section sergeants: Novio, a short, tenacious Filipino; and Pope, a tall, methodical African American. One had a short fuse and the other barely had enough boom to ignite a firecracker. They provided balance.

Unfortunately, one individual resented my methodology. Even though he was in our platoon, he believed I received too much credit for the others winning Soldier of the Month, and he ran a smear campaign to undermine us. I didn't give a flying squirrel's nut what he said or thought. My ship! My way! I wasn't going to make the mistake of catering to anyone's feelings. The soldiers had to decide who to follow, a disgruntled E-4 or an E-7 who had already failed a few times and had a better direction in mind. Winning attitudes prevailed, and eventually all the disgruntled specialist could do was go to the Soldier of the Month board when it was time for his promotion.

All the late nights in the motor pool caused us to uncover several conexes (containers transported by semi-trucks) of equipment. It was too much for one platoon to sort out, so I asked the commander for troop support. A glance inside revealed communication equipment, tools, even live rounds, a total no-go! I requested help from the first sergeant and he casually brushed the request aside. Most of the platoon leaders informed the commander the conexes had been sorted. We took advantage of what we could and made up most of our equipment deficiencies.

One evening, the commander decided to check the conexes. He was so pissed that he had the entire troop in the motor pool searching for equipment reported missing or broken. We left the motor pool well after midnight. The troop's deficiency was reduced by forty percent. We found so much crap that we erased some of squadron's shortages.

Once the commander knew he'd received false reports, I became a trusted adviser. Unfortunately, he wasn't going to Germany with us. He took his talents to law school. By the time the troop finally got on its C-plus game, Outlaw Red (1st Platoon) settled into our standard operating procedures.

Fort Lewis proved to be one of my best assignments. My parents made it a point to visit everywhere we went. Tacoma was no different. In six months, my family visited Victoria Island. We saw two black bears crossing a road on our way to the Pacific Rim. Once I parked the truck, all of us opened our doors except Tia. "Y'all are going out there?" she asked, eyes wider than normal.

"Yes, why not," my mom, stepdad, kids, and I said in unison.

Tia shook her head and locked the doors as we trekked into the fog and greenery of the Canadian woods. The decaying pine-needled floor felt spongy beneath our sneakers. We crossed the forest barrier of mist, and the spruces' scent gave way to a fishy smell as we entered the realm of saltwater and waves slapping against a fossilized beach.

There were aquarium bowls scattered amongst a once-upon-a-time lava flow. Broken seashells at the water's edge added authenticity. Inside the isolated aquariums were urchins and tiny amber-yellow fish that darted under rocks when our shadows passed over the openings. The fish waited for high tide so they could swim to the next bowl a few feet away. It was National Geographic magnificent.

We visited several Seattle tourist attractions; the fish market was the most notable. We went to Mount Rainier. The temperature was nearly seventy degrees as we played in the snow wearing T-shirts. I guess the elevation and ambient air was perfectly balanced, the sun warmed us while the altitude kept the snow crystalline.

The kids found their way atop every waterfall and peered over, giving Tia a conniption fit. They caused my heart to pound too. They acted as if they had been kept in a nest too long and were daring one another to fly. It reminded me of how I used to venture into the woods growing up in Georgia.

When I wasn't exploring the northwest, Outlaw Troop trained for Iraq. The squadron spent a month at Yakima Training Center working on section maneuvers. The platoon was getting dialed in. The first four months at Fort Lewis was balls to the wall. The last two, we made final preparations for our unit move to the farmlands of Bavaria—Vilseck, Germany, to be exact.

The unit did an awesome job preparing our families for the move. The majority of the unit had already obtained European driver's licenses. Our pets didn't have to wait the allotted quarantine period. We went straight into our government quarters, which were furnished until our household goods arrived. Drexler arrived a few weeks before us and had a food basket waiting at our door.

Once the entire platoon was in Germany, my job was easier. Our duty day ended around 1600 hours, while everyone else stood by for leadership to dismiss them well after 1700 hours. As the deployment drew closer, their quitting time got later while ours got earlier. The lieutenant and I planned each week and identified daily tasks that needed to be accomplished. Once those tasks were completed, I sent them home. I didn't care what time it was. Why waste their time when we eyed a fifteen-month deployment?

Between training, my family busted Europe wide open. Venice, Verona, Prague, Baden-Baden, Florence, Paris, Nuremberg, and Neuschwanstein Castle were a few places we visited. We even visited the Flossenbürg and Dachau concentration camps.

Walking through the gates at Dachau, I felt a sluggishness come over me. It was as if the souls that died there still screamed so loudly that the wind carried their echoes. The tour guide showed us where the captives slept and how they started their days. "They started out with a uniform inspection and their uniform buttons were counted. If they had five buttons to start and returned after work with four, they'd be beaten," he told us.

The innocence within my son Ryan came face to face with the ugliness that existed outside of his comprehension. He asked, "For missing a button?" as if his question was asking more questions. The tour guide wiped his brow with a handkerchief and shook his head solemnly.

My soul felt the whisper of a child scream, "Yes, for a button." An acknowledgement that was carried by a breeze. That's when I knew I couldn't protect my children from the world they were about to enter. I had to give them as much knowledge as possible. Of all the spectacular locations we visited throughout Europe, the essence of Dachau carried the loudest echo.

A new group of friends was grafted onto our family tree. The Wings, Shams, and Crills became blood of my blood. Germany was our home. It had to be. Vilseck's cobblestone streets helped place our minds at ease with the fight that loomed ahead. We had no choice but to slow down when driving through town or our steering wheels would shake tremendously because the streets were designed for a slow-paced lifestyle. Empty milk and beer jugs sat outside doors for the deliverymen to collect and replace with freshly brewed and pasteurized libations. Bavarians greeted us with smiles that stemmed from a heritage that existed when 2nd Cavalry was stationed near Nuremburg during World War II.

As training intensified and Iraq drew closer, I saw a trend developing among specific individuals within the platoon. The younger soldiers itched for a combat patch. Not only were they eager to go, but they also seemed like they wanted to see the gore of war. My platoon leader and I brainstormed in our cramped office.

"Sir, why in the world would someone want to go to war?" I asked him. His perspective was seasoned since he had a life, wife, and son prior to commissioning.

"Crazy-young-brainwashed by videogames, I suppose," he said in his whimsical Wisconsin drawl.

The first sight of blood would leave an unhealable scar. Their reason for wanting to go was unknown to me. I believed they idolized war the way young men tend to do. Thinking their invincibility was bulletproof. The so-called fearless ones would become timid, while the choirboys personified bravery. There was nothing heroic about yelling at an Iraqi, "Get the fuck down and don't move! I swear I'll smoke your ass if you blink!"

They suffered from an undiagnosed god complex. Whatever their reasons for wanting to go, it was my job to maintain balance. I knew there was a line we shouldn't cross, and I was determined to keep us toeing that line as 2006 entered the holiday season.

My section sergeants, three of our soldiers, and I toed that line while ninety percent of the platoon took leave stateside. The commander kept asking me if our weapons were cleaned. I should have taken the hint and checked, but I believed my section sergeants when they said the weapons were clean.

Three days into block leave, the commander conducted an impromptu inspection of the arms room. Novio, a handful of helpers, and I stood at attention while the commander grabbed my weapon from me and inspected it for what seemed like five minutes, checking the chamber multiple times. I smirked when he didn't find any dirt or carbon buildup.

"Where's Drexler's weapon?" he asked. I handed it to him. He separated the lower receiver and inserted his finger into its breech. "Dirty," he said, tossing it to me. "Novio, where's your weapon?" the commander's cheeks were turning pink.

"Here, sir," Novio presented it.

He snatched it, held the barrel towards the ceiling and said "This is filthy!" hurling it to my senior scout. "Clean these weapons, Sergeant Lewis!" he said, pointing at me as he stormed to his office.

Novio apologized twice. The NCOs had focused on the soldiers' weapons and neglected theirs. I focused on their word instead of checking them.

"No worries man," I assured Novio. "Pull everything out of the arms room, clean everything, and do 2404s (maintenance forms for deficiencies).

"But, Sergeant Lewis, we already cleaned our night vision and crew-served weapons," Novio said, about to apologize again. Crew-served weapons required two people to fire and involved more cleaning time.

I didn't care. It was my mistake so I cleaned too. I warned the five leave-savers, when the platoon returned, we'd all be introduced to something special.

As promised, when the platoon returned, I smoked everyone on a small hill behind the barracks, including the lieutenant and myself. Smoked was military jargon for physical training to the point of vomiting. I couldn't recall if the other platoons had their weapons tossed back in the same manner as ours were, but they probably didn't command my style of smirk.

Novio and I had been through a few things together. We got attitude from the commander and Command Sergeant Major Rosenthal. During our platoon gunnery after-action review, Rosenthal asked, "What have you been doing this entire time you've been a platoon sergeant?" after we scored mediocre on a preliminary gunnery table.

I despised him for embarrassing me in front of my men. As it turned out, he was relieved for fraternizing with a female staff sergeant who worked in the personnel section. Before he was forced to retire, I requested to use the commander's open-door policy to discuss the unprofessional volleys Rosenthal and I kept lobbing at each other. I informed the first sergeant I wanted to speak with the colonel. My commander who hurled the weapons was apprehensive, but he couldn't prohibit the meeting.

I knocked on the squadron commander's door and let myself in after hearing his permission to enter. I saluted the gregarious Hawaiian and sat at his direction. Augustus was primed to be a CNN military correspondent once he retired.

"What can I do for you Sergeant Lewis?" Augustus asked, grinning unnecessarily.

"Sir, I want to transfer to another squadron."

His eyebrow arched as if his ears had facial lifting mechanisms. I explained all the run-ins and unprofessional vibes I received from Rosenthal. He reassured me I was doing an outstanding job. Said not to worry about the sergeant major.

"Sergeant Lewis, I'm surprised."

"Why, sir?"

"This discussion didn't go the way I envisioned."

"What do you mean, sir?"

"I was told you were not a team player. You are a bit unorthodox, but I like your results," he said while pushing himself from his desk.

"Who said I wasn't a team player, sir"? tilting my head.

He backpedaled from the question. It didn't matter. I went straight to Commander Weapon Hurler and the first sergeant and demanded they explain how I wasn't a team player. They never counseled me or told me directly of their concerns. It was a perfect example of why I hated rubbing elbows with yes-men. Of course, they denied ever saying such a thing. No matter how effective I was at getting results, results didn't matter as much as likability.

Anyway, Novio had my back during all the sergeant major's potshots and gunnery bullshit. "Sergeant Lew, I understand what you're going through and I'm with you," Novio had said at the gunnery table.

He had seen his fair share of the good ole boy system. No other platoon wanted him in their platoons at Fort Lewis. I didn't know what had occurred during his last deployment, but it felt as if he was a scapegoat for something that was better left forgotten. I wasn't afraid to embrace whatever perceived leprosy he had, and he wasn't afraid to stand next to mine.

Regrettably, the spirit of Christmas ended by summer. We entered our final training phase and had our first casualty during a live-fire exercise at Hohenfels Training Center. A young infantryman was accidently shot as he exited his Stryker. It was uncanny timing. He exited the vehicle, turned right, and ran toward his team. The gunner focused downrange. Trigger was pulled as the hero passed the machine gunner's peripheral. Bullet intersected flesh. A mother and father left to deal with terrible timing. I wasn't in the habit of collecting the names of our fallen yet.

Sergeant Jonathon Gilbert, age 22, died at Landstuhl hospital on June 9, 2007. He was training for his second tour of duty to Iraq and earned a Purple Heart surviving a mortar attack during his first tour.

After our training ended, one of my soldiers declared conscientious objector status, which frazzled the platoon. "We don't trust him to have our backs," the consensus spoke.

No matter how much I tried to ease their minds or how many times I said to trust our training. Nothing could calm their anxiety. They projected their fear onto the conscientious objector. We were all afraid as the terror coaster gained momentum.

The command took our objector to Iraq anyway as punishment. For whatever reason, they allowed him to go on Rest and Recuperation (R and R) leave. Obviously, he went absent without leave.

As Iraq loomed closer, Corporal Peterson's friend being dragged through the streets of Mogadishu and images of soldier beheadings plagued my thoughts. Prior to leaving, I purchased an Applegate knife and attached it to my interceptor body armor (IBA) in case we encountered an IED and my weapon was thrown from me; I could use the blade to stab whoever tried to pry me from my Stryker.

As the universe would have it, I didn't leave for Iraq with 1st Platoon. My guys went to Kuwait to upgrade our Strykers with counter-IED equipment, slat armor which added more protection against RPGs and conducted last-minute training.

My family and I left for Colorado Springs for my mother-in-law's funeral. She died in a car accident visiting her husband's grave on a snowy Colorado highway two years to the date of his passing. The last time I had been to Colorado was for his funeral. She had given me some advice then.

"Don't be nobody's hero. Make sure you come home," she coughed while taking a drag from a Pall Mall cigarette as we sat at her kitchen table.

Don't be nobody's hero. America already had too many heroes. Too many names engraved on walls of marble and headstones of granite. Only a few Americans had received a ceremonial flag for their loved one's sacrifice. Only a few clung to memories while clutching medals of valor and Purple Hearts. Soldiers died being heroic for one another, leaving their families to be compensated with fabric dyed blue and stained red for blood. The flag's untouched cotton represented stars. The trade didn't seem fair.

What she was saying was, "Don't be America's hero." She felt that America had handed out enough flags and that she didn't need her daughter receiving one. Sometimes I felt America's flag should have red stars and white and black stripes, but that's a story for someone else to tell.

My mother-in-law didn't want my wife honoring me with her tears. I had come to terms with what I was about to do and what I didn't want to be a part of. I was going because it was my turn. I went with II Chronicles 32:7-8 etched in my heart and my mother-in-law's admonition stenciled on my mind. Iraq was a burial away.

Note 3: The following seven chapters were extracted from the journal I wrote in Iraq. The first entry was written at Forward Operating Base (FOB) Prosperity on August 28, 2007.

BAGHDAD

Outlaw Red

"God created war so that Americans would learn geography."
—*unknown*

In the movie *Fair Game*, the character Joe Wilson, a diplomat who blew the whistle that Iraq was not in possession of WMD, characterized Saddam by saying, "One of Saddam's ministers asked him why he had executed a certain official who was a loyal supporter. Saddam said 'he'd rather kill his friends in error than to allow his enemies to live.' "

I wondered if two monsters could exist on opposite sides of a spectrum? Did one's savagery outweigh a government's abuse of power?

When I arrived in Kuwait, Staff Sergeant Novio was ready to relinquish the platoon. Unbeknownst to Drexler, Novio was furious with him because Drexler overstepped his duties at every opportunity. It was good I returned when I did. Novio had reached a point most soldiers experienced. A point when we asked if cussing out a superior was worth a demotion.

After a few days of being brought up to speed, we flew on a cramped C147s into Baghdad International. A soldier vomited during the flight and the odor of fermented spaghetti wafted through the fuselage. The heat and stench foreshadowed perils that lay ahead.

When he barfed, two more soldiers reached for their barf bags. Their weapons, night vision goggles, protective armor, and CamelBak hydration systems handcuffed their movements, so they overturned their helmets and used them as buckets.

The oversized tires screeched as the plane decelerated on the runway. As we filed off the plane, the heat was arid and piercing. The devil waited by the door and inserted an imaginary blow dryer into our mouths, turning it on high. My lips instantly needed ChapStick, and my throat required ice. We closed our eyes and the blood circulating our eyelids was scorched and washed our vision in crimson.

Once we deplaned, as if on cue, a mortar round impacted the sandy tarmac, a plume of earth powder returned to a sandy mirage. The enemy gave no damns.

From the first moment in country, I knew I wasn't tall enough to be on this freaking roller coaster!

A returning veteran, the first sergeant in fact, laughed and said, "Welcome to Iraq, boys."

I went into a nearby tent, firstly to escape the heat. Secondly, if I was going to die, I didn't want to see it coming. In my mind, the tent provided better protection than the naked sky.

Don't be nobody's hero. My mother-in-law's voice echoed in my head.

When stars replaced Iraq's sapphire sky and night unveiled the city's sparkling streetlights, we took Chinook helicopters into the Green Zone. During the flight, the copilot shot countermeasure flares from the back of the helicopter. I nearly pissed myself and would've jumped six inches if my equipment hadn't kept my butt rooted on the canvas bench. I damn near screamed RPG (grenade), but was glad I didn't.

The calmness of the ramp gunner reassured me I had gambled correctly. He was accustomed to combat antics. The yellow streamer streaked from the chopper turning ambient orange as it swirled toward Baghdad. The Chinook banked left and began descending toward its landing pad. Two combat images in less than twenty-four hours that would've made a bullfrog's hair stand straight. I hoped the next 449 days would be far less soiling.

Forward Operating Base (FOB) Prosperity was an oasis in Baghdad. Division headquarters was situated in one of Saddam's palaces. Aside from a damaged corner, the palace was in pristine condition—marble floors inside, palm trees aligned outside. A huge chunk of the upper portion of stairs was damaged during the initial U.S. airstrikes (shock and awe) that proceeded the invasion. The stairs and corner had since been cordoned off for safety.

The opposite corner and stairs were intact and stepping onto the balcony revealed a picturesque view of canals that fed the vegetation surrounding the palace. The palace was about thirty meters in height. Beyond the palm trees, Saddam was able to watch over the city he once oppressed. The canals were stocked with koi, which was an oddity because one would not associate fish with desert. After seeing it, I noted dictators had a fetish for detail. From what I was taught in school, this was the cradle of civilization. It didn't take a giant leap to see its beauty remained unchanged from ancient times.

From my vantage point, the Iraqi civilians were close-knit, deeply tied by religion, but not wound so tight they couldn't indulge in smoking tobacco. Of course, the Quran could be interpreted in many ways much like the Bible. Christians ate pork while making snap judgments about lesser sins. Muslims, depending on the country, allowed lesser sins to slide, but stoned female rape victims. That's how religion reconciled its overall message of love. It had to have loopholes so we could smite our enemies when necessary.

Iraq was considered a liberal country compared to other Muslim nations. Because the Iraqi Army was disbanded when we invaded, hundreds of thousands of military-age Iraqi men flooded the streets looking for employment. A few profited from illegal activities. Others sold gas at exorbitant prices. Some dug ditches for IED emplacement. Many took a more honest approach, butchering sheep or baking laffa (a native flatbread).

Others were mechanics. Many barely made ends meet. Children migrated to our vehicles whenever we stopped and lowered our ramps. They never tired of peering inside our space ships on wheels. They were so used to danger; foreign soldiers didn't seem dangerous.

Some Iraqi women bore the beauty of Nefertiti while others were heavyset, possibly diabetic. Their swollen, dry ankles were ashen from absorbing dirt from the streets. Even with these imperfections, the beauty of their ancestry was recognizable. The Garden of Eden was somewhere near this city. I didn't have to look hard to imagine the faces of Ruth or Cleopatra. These were their descendants walking by, but no matter who they were or what they did, they were aware when our Strykers drove by.

Our first few days there, the sergeant major's ego ballooned. Sergeant Major Lowery, a Georgia native with a 6' 4" frame who drank sweet tea a little too enthusiastically (not to say he was sweet, but he swore by all things below the Mason-Dixon line and east of the Chattahoochee River) wanted the senior NCOs to convey that the toilets were to remain cleaned at all times. When soldiers took a dump, they were required to use a toilet brush to remove unflushed shit.

"Even though we paid local nationals to clean the latrines?" I asked the first sergeant, who we referred to as Top because he was the most knowledgeable NCO in the troop and relayed the sergeant major's directive.

"Sergeant Major doesn't want to see shit stains in the bowl," Top said emphatically.

"Close your eyes when you take a shit," I mumbled.

Meanwhile, my evaluation was past due. Drexler had it completed prior to block leave in July. I went to the sergeant major on several occasions to remind him I needed it done for the upcoming promotion board. He said he'd look it over soon. I hoped toilet bowls wouldn't distract him from important tasks.

We settled into our tents. The lower enlisted had theirs and the NCOs shared with the lieutenant. Tia's provocative picture and the kid's photos taped to my wall locker were the highlights of our living accommodations.

Before I left Germany, I had given the kids certain chores in order to keep the house running smoothly. Taught them how to drain the water from the washing machine, change air filters, that sort of thing. I requested they send more pictures so I could add more highlights to our drab tent. Tia's perfume-laced letters signed with cherry lipstick helped sanctify life's better moments.

My driver, Sanchy, and Pope helped me build a makeshift chest for my clothes and mementos. The other guys scrounged around the FOB for building materials to make their areas homey. Old WWII-style woolen blankets that once adorned our bunks had been upgraded. Private companies purchased blue comforters to make us feel more at home. A few soldiers used their favorite team blanket. I didn't see any stuffed animals in our tents; however, Sanchy did tape a unicorn to our Stryker as an IED deterrent. Despite sweeping every day, sand drifted onto our plywood floors hourly. The air conditioning kept the 109 degree temperature at bay, but only if we sat next to the one and only vent. Someone was always hogging its coolness.

The dining facility served everything: Mexican, Italian, and Chinese. Cobblers and pies were served every night. It was a skinny man's ideal place to gain NFL weight. The Army-Air Force Post Exchange provided a mini Burger King and Pizza Hut that operated in small trailers near the compact exchange. Soldiers could purchase boots, eye protection, toiletries, muscle milk, and *Playboy* magazines, everything a growing soldier needed to keep his or her mind occupied. I don't recall seeing *Playgirl* magazines for the female soldiers. The army had done one thing right: the food was good.

The first day eating in the mess hall, General Petraeus was on the TV stating he needed more time to evaluate the political landscape and security had improved significantly. In other words, the surge halfway worked. Petraeus was assigned to appease the American public and kick a proverbial can down a never-ending road.

The mess hall buzzed with a different energy. There was a pool party scheduled once stomachs settled. FOB Prosperity was one of Saddam's resorts. Soldiers anticipated frolicking around chlorinated water and relaxing. The pool was situated near a dirt field where soldiers often played flag football or ultimate Frisbee. I skipped the party and reserved my energies for R and R. The outdoor basketball court was near the detainee holding center. We only had to travel a few minutes to get to the U.S. embassy which had upgraded amenities.

On a scale of ten, my first deployment was a two and half. This was a nine-plus.

Our mission entailed assessing security locations. Every critical intersection in our battlespace had either an Iraqi Army or Iraqi police checkpoint. So, to Petraeus's point, they already secured themselves. The checkpoints were differentiated by uniform color. Iraqi police wore black uniforms. Iraqi Army wore fatigues. The Iraqi Army resembled bouncers at a teen nightclub. They lacked discipline. Senior military leaders played both sides. There was an invisible bond between enemy and ally. They could switch alliances with the change of a dollar sign. Hopefully, history would prove me wrong, and Petraeus's speech was right. Every assessment I gathered was that his speech was a farce.

America's government was the best it ever was when it represented a beacon of hope against British oppression. Iraq, on the other hand, lacked beacon qualities. America's path didn't lead to tyranny, as we knew it. Slavery existed and became institutionalized, but tyranny had always been a go-to-war topic, a topic that allowed America to disregard her issues at home and deflect attention to problems abroad. The point being, Iraq was being led by American interests, and not her beacon ideals.

Would Iraq's murkiness filter the effects of Saddam's brutal reign? What would become of her democratic process? What subcategory of its society would slide to the fringes? What made Petraeus think another six months would solve it? The world followed unchanging parallels. America still struggled to resolve issues from its past. Twenty years from now, Iraq may still be dealing with her underlying rifts. Hopefully, none of her problems would become institutionalized. Luckily, Shias and Shiites were of the same color even though they had different perspectives about their Muslim faith. Humans could always find something to quibble over.

Maybe all wars stemmed from man's covetous nature. Men who lived in cardboard boxes coveted one-bedroom apartments. Two rooms became a wish for three, and that desire grew into wanting a home with a pool. Which cultivated visions of mansions, yachts, and oil field expansions, until that unchecked craving created the world we have. One desire after another had us at war with one another. I wondered if it was as simple as stop wanting, and we'd stop warring?

We were fighting against an ideal. No military-minded general would solve Iraq's issue. Iraq's solution resided in humanity's problem.

Playing basketball always helped take my mind off things. My privates challenged me to basketball every chance they got. They would always lose, but my injury-prone back paid the ultimate price. It reminded me of when I was younger, trying to beat my uncle. He played the part of Larry Bird and deemed me Magic. If we weren't playing basketball, it was ghost-man baseball or snowball fights with snow forts. Of course, his fort was built so my lobs fell short and his rained holy hell on me. I think he laced his snowballs with rocks for additional punishment.

When my great-grandmother's apple trees produced fruit, we flung apples at each other. King of the mountain. You name it, we played it. I guess, to my soldiers, I was the unbeatable foe they challenged 100 times for one victory. Funny, Iraq felt familiar.

Walking around the FOB, interacting with dry-cleaning personnel or working out in the palace basement gym, I couldn't escape the unsettledness of being behind walls meant to protect while knowing there were people on the other side ready to harm us. With our technological advances, we were still plagued by tit-for-tat. I wondered if other soldiers felt the weight of history pressing on them the way I did. I imagined the enemy was Genghis Khan reincarnated laying siege to this place. It seemed prison-like, as if I were trapped in a time warp, and war was my warden. I feared the rock of Cain, arrows from the Iroquois, and unseen IEDs. Every aspect of how I could be killed plagued me. War made me fear fleas from rats when all I saw was dogs and cats.

Every time I left our protected square, I felt the dread of every war I'd studied in school. The guards in their overwatch positions resembled war's not-so-distant past. As if they were archers in an Errol Flynn swashbuckler movie. Truthfully, the walls gave us a false sense of security. It's probably why I was able to romanticize about it. I couldn't believe I was fighting in a war.

The first time leaving was surreal. There was a lingering disparity that separated peasants from dictators. The majority of Iraqi civilians lived in squalor compared to the palace. The palace was castle-like. I probably wasn't the only one who felt a king complex. We were liberators and they needed us. Transitioning outside the protected walls never felt right. Subconsciously, I asked, why would a king subject himself to such misery and danger?

I ran into our support platoon sergeant at the small bistro near headquarters. The bistro was set up like a sidewalk coffee shop outside the internet café in a central location on the FOB. Walking to the left under an assortment of shaded trees led to our unit office trailers and the operations center. Farther to the right were our sleeping tents, and to the right of that was the motor pool. Continuing the circle around were the dry cleaners and scrapyard, which lead toward the football field and palace where division headquarters was located. The mess hall, basketball court, and detention center led back toward our unit work area. The center of the FOB was where we could go and feel a little bit of home. The support sergeant sat at an outside table clinching a cup of coffee. He was told he needed to go out and check on logistical operations, chow, and fuel, that sort of thing.

"I'm scared to go out there bro," he confided.

"Do you believe in God's word?" I asked him.

"Yes."

"If you cannot trust the training, trust in His word. I'm afraid too, but our soldiers rely on us to step out that gate every day. If you take the initial step into fear, I promise it will disappear."

I didn't know if I'd made a dent, but all of us first-time deployers were apprehensive about going on patrol. We had to step toward fear and pray we'd make it back. Fear permeated the air. We couldn't survive by holding our breath.

Just as fear gripped our ankles, keeping us from stepping forward, there were other desires that motivated us to jump nose-first into deep ends. A few soldiers violated General Order No. 1, which stated no sex or alcohol. It had only been a few weeks and a married staff sergeant was caught with a female specialist. He ended his career for a soldier who resembled Nanny McPhee. Another couple was caught making a Porta-John slosh. Why they picked a Porta-John to make love in? Maybe because it was one of the few places that could be locked from the inside. Most soldiers had a roommate or lived in a twenty-person tent.

Depending on how tidy the stalls were, the Chuck Norris jokes written on the walls lightened the day. Something as simple as "Chuck Norris was the reason why Waldo was in hiding" spiced the day. Another shithouse poet wrote, "20 more days till we get extended." Must've been a soldier close to the 365th day.

At the height of the surge, soldiers had been involuntarily extended for an additional three months. A unit from Fort Lewis made it all the way home, debarked the aircraft, and was held in a hanger for a few hours. Their extension orders were issued after they had taken off. They only got to kiss their spouses. Not even a quick conjugal and they were back in flight to the wonderful Middle East. A terrible joke, but an even funkier kind of love.

We usually pulled quick reactionary force (QRF) at command outpost (COP) Ramagen. On rare occasions, we pulled QRF at the FOB. This instance we did it at the

FOB while a few soldiers hung out at the trucks monitoring radios, a few played video games or slept. Everyone hoped we didn't get alerted. An alert meant something significant happened.

The COP was far less accommodating than the FOB. The building had belonged to Saddam's sister. A nice pad on a Tigris riverbank with a view into Sadr City. The Bible came alive there. From where we parked, I could throw a stone and make a Mesopotamian river splash. It was an unforgettable classroom setting.

Sadr City crackled with gunfire constantly. Sometimes at night we witnessed amber tracer rounds laser-beaming their way to potential insurgents. Occasionally, we heard the ping of sniper fire impacting our building, so I advised the guys to stay behind cover whenever they went to the roof to smoke.

Inside the foyer, a stairwell had been damaged during shock and awe. Three stairs were broken approximately fifteen feet up. It was broken in such a way that only one person could go up or down at that juncture. We must have looked like mountain goats negotiating the damaged spot.

Upstairs were the sleeping quarters with bunk beds. Downstairs was our operations room. A trailer served as a latrine. Another for showers. About fifty meters away stood a garage structure headquartering Iraqi police. The Iraqis were not allowed in our operation area for security reasons.

It was counterproductive being at the COP. They wanted us out in sector for quick response even though the FOB was less than two miles away. This was the "winning hearts and minds" strategy. We needed to be embedded with the population. In reality, one platoon pulled sentry duty, another patrolled, while another reset at the FOB. We could run all operations from the FOB; let the police command the COP and nix sentry duty altogether because we weren't embedded at the outpost either. Only the platoon that patrolled was.

The outpost became an ideal place to write because it didn't have many distractions except for the kittens that lived under the latrine. Four furballs entertained me like a Bob Hope United Service Organization (USO) show. I pictured them wearing straw hats and tap shoes as they tumbled over one another biting their siblings' ears. The mother was content letting her brood around us. They never ventured far from her meow. When nothing was going on, I sat and watched them aimlessly.

The runt's neck had the strength of an overcooked noodle. He could barely lift his head to suckle his mother's nipple. His siblings pranced on top of him stamping out whatever energy he clung to.

When a soldier jerked, the mother and her strong dashed for safety, leaving the runt exposed near the dugout's entrance. His hunger pangs deepened.

Now, it seems inhuman to have watched it vanish. Hard to accept how I lacked compassion. I should have taken it to the river and ended its suffering. Instead, I identified with the strong.

After a couple of days passed, all the kittens were missing. Had a soldier used them for target practice? Given the vibes I got from some of the men, I would have bet a large sum that that was what happened. Some people itched to discharge their weapons. Maybe they knew there was a sniper across the river waiting to do us harm. Or because the canines that scavenged over the garbage heaps didn't stand a chance when certain platoons drove by.

The sergeant major came to check on us at the COP. He reiterated that he would pull Sergeant First Class Dailey and me in January or February to make room for the newly promoted E-7s. I wanted to stay Outlaw Red, but wearing the body armor inflamed my herniated disc. It was unbearable standing for hours in the Stryker hatch waiting for Alpha Section to return from their dismounted patrols. Desk work might not be so bad. I told the platoon back at Vilseck about the transfer. They were disappointed, but I'd been preparing them for months.

Every time we left the COP, we reconnoitered routes to the combat hospital (CASH), which was in the Green Zone. The surgeons at the CASH did one hell of a job stabilizing the severely wounded for transport back to Landstuhl, Germany for more lifesaving surgeries. Buddy-aid and the combat medic were the first steps in that life-saving chain.

If we ever got hit, it was my responsibility to make sure we made it there ASAP; therefore, every driver had to be able to get us there without being directed. I wanted to eliminate as many points of failure as possible.

Around the second week, we conducted left-seat rides which allowed us to acclimate ourselves to combat by observing the outgoing unit. The following week was right-seat rides. The outgoing unit observed and advised while we conducted combat missions.

The outgoing platoon was from 2-14 Cavalry, which transitioned to 2nd Brigade Fort Lewis, Washington after 1st Brigade reflagged. They were led by Sergeant First Class Richardson. His appearance hadn't changed since we did basic training in 1994. He was still bald, and his smile appeared bright against his sun-absorbing complexion.

AREA OF OPERATIONS

Sergeant First Class Richardson (Rich) platoon mission was to support the security forces as well as the local hospital while gaining influence with local leaders. Building a relationship allowed us to search for insurgents without instigating backlash.

During the second week, Rich's platoon showed us our area of operation (AO), or battlespace, Iraqi security forces locations and checkpoints, the hospital and its generator. He also introduced us to the imam—the neighborhood leader, and showed us the evac routes to the CASH (hospital). The AO was metropolitan. Lots of pedestrians and cars idling at stoplights with an occasional donkey-drawn cart hauling local produce or a butchered lamb.

The third week Rich's platoon transitioned to an observatory role. The final week, they prepared to return home, and we owned fifteen city blocks of Iraqi battlespace.

Shortly after we took over the right-seat phase, we heard an explosion that rivaled a volcano's grumble. Everyone's neck twisted in its direction as we familiarized ourselves with tiny spider alleys that intertwined our northern sector. The soldier's first reaction was to course toward the calamity. I calculated the distance and determined it was outside our area of responsibility. When the question was raised if we were going to investigate, I kept their attention picking beans from our hill. Rich nodded in approval.

Rich was on his second tour of duty and survived two IED attacks. The first occurred during his first deployment. The second happened shortly after his arrival to the area we patrolled which gave the war an ominous intimacy. The second IED sent him to Walter Reed Hospital in Washington, D.C., obviously, he recovered quickly and returned to finish the mission.

As we familiarized ourselves in Baghdad, Rich told me a story about an Iraqi man and his son. The son injured himself while playing near a construction site. He fell ten or fifteen feet and a piece of rebar separated his bicep muscle from the humerus bone. The father came to Rich's platoon seeking medical assistance. Unfortunately, the wound was several days old. Rich's lieutenant requested the boy be taken to the CASH. Their squadron commander denied his request. Rich never gave a reason why the commander had denied it.

His platoon medic patched the kid's arm as best he could. The following day, the medic redressed it. Rich's lieutenant said if they saw the boy again, they would disobey orders and take him to the CASH. Rich said the area was relatively quiet now compared to what they'd encountered earlier.

My heart sank a little hearing about the boy. I never asked what happened to him. I had an overwhelming feeling the kid died because of his injury. Rich's voice had a heaviness in it when he told us. There didn't seem to be any hope for any runt when it came to Iraq.

Sanchy was an easygoing Texan with a heart larger than his state. He quietly said, "That's messed up," from a headset in the hull below. Sanchy peered over the driver's shoulder to see how he maneuvered the vehicle.

Soldiers at the frontline had to deal with political slogans that didn't quite mesh with realities on the ground. Had I not written that story, I might've forgotten it.

Rich implied that money influenced decisions. Generals said *win hearts and minds*, but when the opportunity arose, our hands were tied. The bigger issue was that Iraqis didn't trust their government, nor was it capable of taking care of civil issues. So it didn't matter what we did. Or how much security we provided. Iraqis' frustrations could easily be focused back on us.

I asked Rich how the Iraqis felt about Saddam.

He said, "They hated him, but at least they had running water, electricity, and waste disposal," and finished by telling his to driver to put some distance between the truck in front of us. His driver sped up to avoid a mountain of garbage then slowed down to complete Rich's guidance. Those heaps were ideal for concealing IEDs, and trash was everywhere. After a couple of weeks swerving around the heaps, our noses were accustomed to Iraq without Saddam Hussein.

I couldn't say the streets were less bloody. Saddam was a Sunni. Once he was captured, Shias, a different type of Muslim, sought retribution against Sunni elites. An undercurrent of civil war was unleashed when we overthrew his regime. Secretary of State Colin Powell warned Bush that invading Iraq would be like breaking a piece of crystal, and we would own every broken piece.

Many soldiers deployed knowing what winning hearts and minds meant, but we failed at it because simple execution was not fully funded. We always seemed to gain a heart while losing a mind, or save a soul while destroying a heart. The boy's mangled arm reminded me that we didn't bring enough glue to fix what we broke.

I had my first real interaction with some of the kids in the affluent part of our sector and wrote some prose once I returned to base.

Iraqi Girl,

Before I left Germany, my daughter, Diamond, gifted me a dinar to buy something while in Iraq. The money was worthless to me. I started to give it back, but kept it to give to a girl in Iraq that reminded me of my daughter. I thanked my daughter and went to war with an indifferent stance. A few days went by and that dinar slipped my mind; however, one day I remembered to take the money. While on patrol, I reached in my pocket and tossed the money from my Stryker to an Iraqi girl who was passing by. At the time, the little girl was by herself. She was puzzled as to why I had thrown the money. She was maybe eight years old. She ran behind the combat vehicle trying to return my daughter's gift. "No. It is yours to keep," I said, waving my hands frantically for her to stay away.

Her eyes grew large with amazement when she understood. Americans threw money away on whims. I didn't give any thought to her surroundings. What an idiotic gesture. These people gave hugs and kisses when greeting. As she turned to go home to show her family her prize, a boy saw her waving her money triumphantly. He hit her and stole her money. I was furious. Mad at the boy. Mad at myself. It wasn't my war. It wasn't hers either. War was man's ignorance. I let her and my daughter down as my vehicle rolled away.

Richardson laughed knowing it was my first deployment and little things were still heartbreaking. Combat training was nothing like combat. We couldn't mimic emotional realism. Emotions had their own heaviness. Training was over and choices had magnified consequences.

Across the Tigris River, 3rd Squadron got into skirmishes. The enemy probed them for weaknesses. Despite the contrast of slums and high-rises, Baghdad was a city of distinction. As dangerous as it was, it was beautiful seeing how the people interacted with one another. I saw a tall blond-haired albino weaving his way in and out of a river of olive faces as if he belonged swimming through the middle of them. None of the other colored faces acknowledged his presence, but I was aware of the beautiful strangeness that existed. I examined every oddity.

Some U.S. soldiers looked at Iraqis as dogs that scavenged over trash heaps. They didn't outright say it, but their actions revealed it. One particular patrol we conducted toward the end of right-seat phase proved this point.

Charlie One-Four (me) and One-Three (Pope), the respective call signs of Bravo Section, were positioned west on an east-running alley. Charlie One-Two (Novio) and One-One (Drexler) made up Alpha Section. They were 300 meters east blocking traffic from entering an affluent neighborhood in the southern portion. When citizens noticed us, they backtracked promptly, but one disheveled man didn't. A voice crackled in the headset: "Red-Four this is Red-One Delta-over."

"This is Red-Four, send it," I replied from the rear Stryker hatch, watching a boy guide a donkey-drawn cart past my war chariot.

"We have a guy refusing to turn around—over." A long pause. "Never mind, we took care of it."

"Roger," I replied as two Iraqi women walked by leisurely following the path of boy and donkey. The weight of my combat gear weighed on my injury-prone back. I wanted to exit the vehicle and walk around instead of standing in a hatch for three motionless hours. When we returned to base, I heard what happened during the pause.

Earlier in the mission, that disheveled man tried to enter Bravo's cordon. One-Three's gunner waved at a passerby to communicate to the man that it was not safe to come near us. Several arm grabs and sidesteps and the helpful Iraqi managed to corral the man away. We noticed the man's mental capacity was diminished and appreciated the Iraqi's intervention, especially considering al-Qaeda used mentally challenged people as suicide bombers.

An hour later, the man had made his way to Alpha Section. One-One's gunner didn't have a helpful Iraqi to intervene. His solution was to shoot the man with a non-lethal shotgun round.

The news was relayed by Red-Three (Staff Sergeant Pope). Pope listened to the events as described by Billy Badass, aka Red-One's gunner, in the lower enlisted tent. Everyone laughed and gave Billy congratulatory praise. "You the man," they said. "Serves that motherfucker right."

Nelly served as my gunner. He was a surfer from a mountainside California town. He and Sanchy witnessed the events unfold on the western end and said the man was nonthreatening and didn't need to be treated like that. They encountered war's fine line. I couldn't say one was right and the other wrong. The issue was viewing the man as less than. In theory, Billy wasn't wrong, but I wished they hadn't enjoyed it so much.

I learned the Iraqis had two options: help U.S. soldiers find bad guys in exchange for a working generator (electricity), or die at the hands of bad guys for talking to us. Darkness or death? We talked to them regardless, placing them in a terrible predicament. What would I choose if I was them?

Second Squadron handed out pamphlets that stated we were there to help, while the enemy hung posters in Sadr City that read "Support your local militia." Soldiers went out in sector with the sole purpose of removing propaganda.

"If we see these posters again, we'll take away the generator and the money to fix the school," a civil affairs officer said as he attempted to strong-arm an imam.

It was a no-win situation. A lot of good men had to die for the rest of them to enjoy a few hours of electricity because the generator only ran at certain times. One neighborhood was able to see, while others lived in darkened squalor. Bullets or peace were the only choices on the menu.

Were we going about this the right way? Would you openly help your liberators when there's so much bullshit going on behind the scenes? Kill one dictator only to plot against the next one standing in line? Their choices were precariously costly. Their trusting in us meant we had a duty to protect them. Everyone knew we could only partially fulfill that obligation. We couldn't stay in sector indefinitely, but the enemy could.

It was one of our last days conducting right-seat phase and the morning zipped with activity as the temperature rose. Several platoons converged in the motor pool, preparing for their missions as we left for ours. The first moments were filled with laughs. Wilson fell into a puddle of sewage water. The hole looked shallow and long enough to hold Willy's 6'3" stature, but deep enough to hide a Winnebago. When he stepped in it, his momentum carried every inch of him into the baptismal sludge.

Ostertag laughed, which infuriated Willy. He was already pissed because Ostertag had been aggravating him all morning. Willy damn near broke Ostertag's nose. Sanchy did his best Smokey impression and said, "You got knocked the fuck out." All we did was laugh. We all wanted to punch Ostertag at one time or another.

Usually, the stench traveled through our nostrils and punched our uvulas, provoking a gag reflex. Days later, Willy's throat convulsed like he was still trying to vomit away the memory.

The mission ended by noon, which allowed us to eat at the mess hall. Novio huffed and stabbed his fork into his potatoes whenever Pope spoke.

"What's bothering you?" I asked.

"Sergeant Pope, you gotta move faster man," Novio began.

"Uh, what's the problem?" Pope used vocal fillers which added to his deliberateness.

Those two went back and forth while I finished my plate and grabbed Novio's chocolate pie because he wasn't going to eat it. Pope defended the indefensible. He did march at a slower pace than the rest of us; however, nobody beat him when it came to attention to detail.

Novio was a hard-charging scout whose heat dial sometimes needed to be lowered.

We ended lunch with me calming Novio down and reassuring Pope that our fifteen-month finish line hadn't changed.

The following day I chose to laugh at Novio's frustration instead of intervening. Alpha Section finished their equipment layout before Bravo. I sat on my Stryker ramp, swatted flies, and waited to see if he would assist Bravo. He didn't, so Alpha Section did a few pushups before the day got too hot. Couldn't have Novio so upset that he wasn't willing to help his buddy.

Later that afternoon we finished our equipment layout and returned to our semi-cool tents. I stopped by the dry cleaners to grab my laundry since it was on the way. Other platoons still rearranged items as we left. We should have lent a hand, but there was a difference in moving slowly and not progressing. Nothing much had changed since Fort Lewis. I was never upset at my peers like Novio was at Pope. Plus, I would have only added another chief to a situation that had too many chieftains.

The biggest issue seemed to be settling the lieutenant's nerves. He couldn't stay out of enlisted business. It aggravated Novio. It was in an officer's DNA to want to have their hands on every aspect. It was their job to know everything. Consequently, his meddling worked in my favor because it united Pope and Novio.

Drexler put out information before it went through the NCO common-sense test. For instance, I was in charge of staffing. Before I could issue a roster, he would publish one. Pope must've felt frustrated because he finally voiced his concern.

"Uh, Sergeant Lew, can I bend your ear?" he asked.

"Shoot," I replied.

"Um–yeah, the LT has three of the four senior NCOs on one truck. What if that truck gets hit? Who was going to take charge?" His question was perfectly timed with an exhale.

I simply deleted his and implemented mine. Of course, I explained my reasoning to Drexler. He was always open to advice. It was something I learned from Fort Hood: delete and redo. Nothing was set in stone.

"The section sergeants think of you as their new platoon sergeant, sir," I said. It was meant to be a joke. I continued, "There are times when the NCOs will drop the ball, and that's when you can crush our nuts. Until then, relax and enjoy the NCO show, sir."

The point was taken, and he released the reins. A platoon sergeant's duty was a balancing act that replicated painting a Picasso. My boss, the lieutenant (LT), had to make mistakes to learn; but he couldn't make so many that he gets himself fired. And it wasn't an equation weighted toward success. He could do a hundred important things right, and one momentous move wrong, and we could all face prison or worse. I had to allow him to throw paint on a canvas and hoped the picture turned out brilliantly. Frustrating for the NCOs, because most times we didn't have the patience to allow the process to finish.

During dinner chow, we exited the motor pool and went to dinner to debunked the rumor mill. We heard we would be in Sadr City in six months. The fighting was nonstop there. Good army officers gravitated toward a fight. The consensus was that Augustus jockeyed for action in Sadr City. Me being a low man looking up, officers lived to outdo their predecessors. If Patton did x, y, and z, the next man had to do that plus three. Making my soldiers go to Soldier of the Month boards was like Augustus wanting us to go help 2nd Squadron. The idea of being memorialized for the sake of historical supremacy made me appreciative for only needing to do "x" and nothing else.

Our patrol schedule reflected our commander's desire to find bad guys. Sometimes the schedule had us doing one patrol a day, most times it was two or three. This particular September day we went back in sector for a third time an hour after dinner. The platoon heard a report about an IED explosion near the FOB, which spiked their anxiety levels. Even though these explosions became more frequent, our discipline slipped as we grew accustomed to hearing them.

They said the deadliest time was the first and last thirty days. The first, because we didn't know the area or the enemy; the latter, because we would get too relaxed. The minute we got comfortable with Green Zone pool parties was when the enemy would bust our heads open.

The first thing my medic, Stanley, a Native American Minnesotan, did was take his Kevlar off. I chewed his ass. Couldn't help thinking if this was day seventeen, what would happen on day 405? What's crazy was all the gung-ho soldiers who wanted to deploy had reservations about going into Sadr City. Funny, how the world spun.

The three-mission day afforded us an easy day. I peeked into the lower enlisted tent and saw Sanchy cleaning his weapon, so I cleaned mine. After that, LT and I planned out some training.

We ran scenario-based training sometimes when we returned to base. "Two truck has been hit; all crew are litter urgent," I transmitted over the radio.

Alpha Section halted because the two-truck led. Bravo Section secured a perimeter while Stanley ran to render aid. Drexler sent a fictional MEDEVAC request over the platoon radio frequency. I hopped out with dismounts and attached tow cables to the two-truck and we continued to the motor pool and conducted an after-action review. I made sure the next platoon sergeant would be in good hands.

During our refit day, the troop misplaced a PQ2 laser sight which mounted on an M4 rifle. Eventually, they discovered it had been turned in months ago. After it was found we conducted physical training. Many soldiers ran into problems when they returned home because the entire time on deployment, they failed to maintain weight standards. I didn't want that to happen to us. The soldiers bitched of course, but the flying squirrel was still performing acrobatic tricks with his balls. Therefore, I handed out "Cry Me a River" concert tickets.

The two other platoons relaxed on their refit days. I rarely, if ever, relaxed. Preparation and establishing a routine were how I coped with fear. That approach probably drove Drexler crazy. He always broke the no smoking on the vehicle rule. That frustrated Novio and me because it was his soldiers who asked "but why" after everything we said. I relented by letting him smoke as long as he sold the same "Cry Me a River" tickets and told the soldiers they couldn't smoke. In the end, he outranked me, and I tried to ignore whenever he let his crew into the concert for free. Be wrong together was the first rule for a reliable platoon leader and sergeant relationship and we acted as one.

In preparation for Ramadan, we conducted more night raids. It was almost midday, and I hadn't been asleep. Sergeant Brown made it worse when he informed me the Iraqi Army had been hit with an IED. I was bombarded with when would we get hit?

Disrupted sleep and back pain gnawed at my ability to function. Oftentimes, I compensated by making Sanchy watch the front of the vehicle while Nelly traversed the turret to the rear. I retreated inside the truck, evading the sun for even hotter shade. I'd pass out for a short while. Sweat would pool in my gloves. After twenty minutes, I rotated in, struggling to keep my eyes open while standing. I dreaded standing. My back would spasm. Depending on the mission, Stanley sometimes staged with our vehicle. When he did, he was placed in rotation.

I thought it would take us longer to get as comfortable as we did. To me, comfort equaled danger, so I wanted to avert indiscipline. But I was probably the biggest violator by not resting properly prior to missions.

In addition to me not resting, privates played mom-and-pop games with the newly promoted sergeants. Ask mom because dad always says no sort of thing.

My broad guidance may have contributed to the communication gap between section and first-line supervisors. Plus, the soldiers knew the LT said, "yes" to everything when he was given a cigarette.

I wanted to create a free-thinking environment. I didn't care how the sergeants got the job done as long as it was done. However, junior NCOs needed a more direct leadership style. It was something we needed to address.

Novio attend more platoon sergeant meetings in preparation for my departure. I encouraged him to be more vocal during platoon mission planning. If his plan was solid, we went with it. I needed him to be the platoon's continuity. All and all, things ran smoothly until they didn't.

Army gremlins attacked us right before we departed for a 0700 mission. We stayed up until 0200 hours fixing our radios and tracking systems. As we staged at the gate, Red-Three's coms sounded garbled. Red-One could radio squadron, but he couldn't be heard by Red-Two, or myself.

Drexler's request to stand-down was granted. The commander allowed us to coordinate with Richardson's platoon. They were almost packed and ready to leave. If they hadn't squared us away, we would have been out of luck. Their communication guy schooled our guy on some deficiencies we overlooked.

Once we fixed our radios, we rolled to the COP to test the range of our comms, and have a discussion about the last three missions to identify things we did right and issues we could improve. Sergeant Demerit, our dismounted leader, asked, "Who doesn't take this seriously?"

Apparently, McDonald, aka D-Nasty, exited the truck without a magazine in his weapon. Actually, the magazine somersaulted out of his weapon and onto the ramp. Our Strykers were quiet as a kitten's purr. They were perfect scouting vehicles in that regard. When the ramp was lowered, it had a low hiss and a sound-proof thump when its lip hit the pavement. D-Nasty's magazine clanging down a ramp when we staged for a raid at a nearby house wasn't the sound Demerit was expecting. D-Nasty wasn't the only one having a Barney Fife moment.

We rolled out with our counter-IED jammer equipment turned off. The device blocked cellular signals to prevent IED initiation. If we found mistakes before the enemy did, it was a win. No matter what we did, it was a game of chance.

The enemy waited to make us pay for our stupidity. Becoming complacent was easy. Our battlespace seemed tranquil, but there was something sinister lurking. An IED could be placed anywhere. The real fear was continuously wondering where it might be, so the guessing meant the enemy had effectively implanted one inside me.

Rich's platoon was gone, and I was left wondering which one of our failures would be our saddest regret.

MISSING HOME

"The true soldier fights not because he hates what is in front of him, but because he loves what is behind him." —G.K. Chesterton

We spent most of the day planning a snag and grab mission later that night. Once planning was done, I retrieved the journal from beneath my mattress and settled my head onto a feathered pillow. A sharp feather calamus jabbed my neck as the air-conditioning whined as it kept pace with the heat outside. I engaged the pen's tip and delved into thoughts of home.

The feather end brought back memories of family camping trips during chilly Ohio autumns. The first bluegill I snagged. Its tiny body jiggled at the end of the line and my dad's jubilation as he fanned the Polaroid capturing our moment.

I had taken my sons fishing at Fort Knox. We had a lot of nibbles but didn't catch anything. I baited the hooks wrong. In a sense, we wasted our time, but not really. Hopefully, they'd remember the attempt rather than the fact we only caught lake weed.

As a kid, my aunts, uncles, and cousins would be arrayed around a campfire's glow. Aunt Bella would start the first horror story as we dangled hot dogs over a crackling fire. Uncle Randy took swigs from a thermos.

I scratched my neck and adjusted my pillow. I miss hayrides with my cousins.

It was during quiet moments that I realized how much military families sacrificed. Constantly on the go. Running from mission to mission, duty station to duty station. For all the things my dad had gotten wrong, he had the attempt right.

The army was filled with soldiers who said they couldn't wait to do this or that when they got out. Most of us had put off our dreams until our military service ended. By that time, the best years were missed opportunities. I needed to change to a present-day way of thinking. I was always focused on the next promotion or the next move up.

When I was stationed at Fort Knox in 2003, my buddy and I traveled to Indianapolis to check our promotion records. Long story short, I found that my Department of the Army photograph hadn't been updated. We returned to Fort Knox with our files as perfect as could be. Both of us made the E-7 list. We celebrated his promotion at his house because he was promoted first.

When my number hit, we threw an epic party at my house. People brought bottles of Hennessey, my drink of choice. Depending on the storyteller, I drank three bottles. Impossible, but out of seven bottles, three were empty.

Around 2200 hours, the fellas decided to visit the NCO club. Tia was passed out on the couch. The other spouses straightened up and played cards. The men maneuvered to the club in our grass-cutting garb and continued downing shots and beer with promotional cheer.

Now, as a drunk I am talkative and sometimes wet-eyed emotional. My battle buddy who had been promoted two months earlier found me sobbing on a barstool. The depressant made me depressed about how I had treated Tia. "Knock that crap off and drink up!" my buddy warned, nearly slapping me off the stool.

A few minutes later, without informing him, I darted out into the Kentucky air and ran home as fast as my drunken state allowed. It was more trotting and zig-zagging that soon turned into hobbling.

In order to get home faster, I took a shortcut through a field surrounded by a chain-link fence. A sober person would have walked around the fence, but an intoxicated man goes over it. The reason why alcohol was an effective killer was it made smart people stupid. As I reached my left foot over the barbs, my other foot slipped. Like the Iraqi kid, my ankle was impaled. I was stuck spread-eagle dangled on the fence. Right foot tip-toed the ground while blood trickled down my left leg. I attempted to free myself twice, and debated whether to give up.

What if military police (MP) drove by and found me like this? What if they didn't come and the churchgoers find me dangled like an impromptu crucifix? *What an idiot* drummed in my head as adrenaline percolated through my veins. The warm blood trickling toward my groin had turned cold by the time I hoisted my foot free. I surveyed the damage and avoided further shortcuts.

I arrived to a cleaned house. My wife still slept on the couch as I limped to the bedroom. A knock drummed on the front door. Was it the MPs? Had they followed my blood trail home? Tia answered the door. It was the buddy I left at the bar mumbling that he lost me and had no idea where I had gone.

"He's here," she said.

"What!? That muther..." More bumbling as he foraged through the refrigerator, made a to-go plate, and headed home.

The scar on my ankle is a great reminder to remain humble. When my kids do foolish things, I can rub my scar and keep my mouth shut.

I placed the journal under my pillow. Dampness from back sweat made the light-blue comforter darker. I walked under the shade trees to headquarters and grabbed our mail. The officers discussed strategy and battle plans. The first sergeant leaned against a wall sipping coffee and nodded. I acknowledge him, grabbed the mail satchel and exited.

I returned to my bunk and wrote some more. My eldest son was on my mind. Good kid. Maybe I caused him unnecessary pain because I wasn't ready to be a father when we met. He was barely two and I was barely twenty-two when I entered his world. I was figuring out what it meant to be a man. No one laid out a blueprint. I followed a traditional plan: graduate high school, go to college, find a job, and get married. Christians were supposed to get with Christians. Muslims got with Muslims. But the truth was, we gravitated toward people without gravitating to ourselves first.

This would be my advice to him: between the ages of eighteen and twenty-eight, explore the world. Find yourself. If you can, unhinge yourself without breaking yourself. Find the limits of what you can handle;

understand past hurts that motivate you in misguided directions. Rebuild yourself. Establish your likes, dislikes, and compromises and write them down. Find people who have done the same unhinging and rebuilding and list-making and compare notes. Know yourself intimately before becoming intimate. Merge the known with the unknown, then marry someone who has learned how to be married with themselves. That type of marriage with one's self didn't occur until our forties, if ever.

I hoped he surpassed me the same way I wanted to surpass my dad. As I got older, there was no real separation between my father and me. I was like him like my sons were replications of me.

My father prepared me for life's tough times. It was a difficult adjustment after my parents divorced as a nine-year-old. I remember he came home to gather some essentials. He sat me on a sofa that belonged on *Sanford and Sons* and apologized for his failures as a man. For many years, I couldn't reconcile the disdain I felt when he ripped himself away from us. Many of the lessons he taught wouldn't manifest until I became a man bouncing from relationship to relationship, learning from my bruises.

"I love your mother dearly. When you get married, love your wife better than I did your mother. Why do you think my marriage failed?" he asked.

It was the first time he asked a question where I didn't feel an impulse to lie. "You didn't love each other anymore," I said.

"It failed because I didn't put God first." His chin absorbed tears as he squeezed his cheek stubble against my forehead. I surmised men should put God first.

There was a great deal more instruction I wasn't given. Even so, I felt his love occasionally even though he always loved me. I hoped my children would come to understand that I love them constantly no matter how many inconsistencies I unintentionally showed them. We tended to overlook how much forgiveness is required when loving.

Tia's provocative photograph appeared to wink at me from my wall locker. Damn, her eyes had a Mona Lisa effect. Her picture always brought my prose to life. Recalling when I took her to Jekyll Island late one night while stationed at Fort Stewart, Georgia.

Remember When My Love,

Remember those times when we made love on a beach? We had taken a late-night stroll on a sandy shore. Salt marinated the air. Waves dashed against our innocence. Hearts thumped offering an invitation for unspoken bliss.

When the door opened, was your soul cajoled or did you go with the natural order of things, stopping just shy of sin? Did you die a little from living intensely? Were you thankful afterwards?

Why did love always conflict with what it is and what ought to be? Love required an intellectual kind of feeling, because love faltered along reconciliatory lines.

Two of love's best moments were at night when you laid your head on my chest; and in the morning when we woke side by side. My natural order rushed against your spiritual levy. Slowly, chipping away your holy undoing. Each give and receive gave way to soulful hallelujahs. We drifted back to sleep and dreamt of waking to another amen. If that was sin, let me pay my penance now so I could have happiness and actively pursue it. Carry me to judgment because I shall forever want this.

Remember those moments, meaningful and wonderful; broken and confused; makeups after emotional wrecks; pleasant sweet nothings that solicited pillow talk meanderings. Held hands as we drove to no place particular. Your eyes glistened with a familiar tear. Was it happiness? If it was, the end of your wet trail was where my heaven began. Remember when, my love? I missed the intimacy that freedom provided.

I went to the internet café and checked my email. The internet was slow, but it beat my first deployment to Kuwait, where I had to stand in line for hours to use a Morale, Welfare and Recreation telephone to call home.

My wife and daughter had written. Tia wrote that some spouses were having issues with their husbands and she was filling a counselor's role. We were barely weeks into the deployment and soldiers questioned their spouse's whereabouts. Worse yet, some soldiers had to be escorted to the phone center to put their wives' minds at ease because they hadn't called home since they departed. During my email correspondence, I wrote that I would call Tia after midnight when the phone center was less busy.

My daughter shared a few passages from her journal. Her teacher encouraged her to write her feelings to help her cope with the deployment. Her writing was quite astonishing. I wish I still had access to my military email to share one.

After dinner, I studied maps of our territory and dozed off with a map teepeed on my chest. Upon waking, I walked to the phone center and called Tia. I spent several minutes listening to a busy signal. I walked back to the tent to grab my phone book for her cell number. It was busy too. She had two phone lines jammed. Her email of other people's issues became my issue. The vein in my neck was probably bulging by the time I read the calling instructions attentively. I dialed 0049 instead of 01149.

By the time I had her on the phone, I fell victim to preliminary speech and forgot to lead with her picture winking at me and our Jekyll Island excursion. A few minutes into her explaining her day, the indirect fire warning blared. It sounded like a tornado siren whenever radar picked up incoming mortar or a rocket attack. I told her I would instant message after the all-clear alarm.

The nearest concrete bunker had six soldiers hunkered under it. I squeezed in with them. The bunker walls were about eight inches thick and shaped like an overturned U. Each bunker could house eight people and they were spread sporadically around the FOB. It was supposed to offer better protection than soft-skinned tents or aluminum trailers.

As the months dragged on, the alarms steadied, but the amount of people that scurried to cram inside lessened. Eventually, the conclusion was drawn that it was better to die comfortable than scurrying like an insect. Inside the bunker, I became familiar with false alarms and how war invaded intimate spaces. After the all-clear, I spent the next hour instant messaging Tia X-rated longings.

Instant messaging had been a small blessing. It was easier to write my feelings than to speak my mind. Most times, I didn't want to offend or be misunderstood. I enjoyed revealing more of myself to her. Oftentimes, I wanted to say, "Hey beautiful," or some other term of endearment, but never did. A deep-rooted weed choked my vocal cords.

On my way back to the tent I saw Ostertag dashing around a corner. I heard a rumor that he and his buddy found an Iraqi lady who batted her eyes and laughed at his corny jokes. Some of the NCOs warned him that she was probably gathering intel from him. With more and more soldiers getting into trouble and Ostertag's track record with women, I needed to keep tabs on his whereabouts.

Back at the tent, I finished writing. If I fixed me (being open), would it result in her happiness? That's the crux of a relationship; we needed inner joy in order to influence someone else's outward happiness. I winked at Tia's picture and slept for an hour before executing a 0400 mission. The mission entailed circling our territory's perimeter twice then staging at the railyard for thirty minutes to demonstrate our presence.

Sun shined on Iraq before the roosters crooned. I was tired and needed sleep before we executed a mission later that afternoon.

I read a few passages in the Bible, jotting some sentiments before dozing off. Obligation and dedication had been on my mind. Obligated meant compelled or constrained. Dedicated meant committed or enthusiastic. Husband and wife should be obligated to one another enthusiastically. Did people stay together for obligatory reasons? Maybe relationships failed because people felt constrained rather than compelled, and committed rather than enthusiastic. If we attained the first definition of obligated (compelled) and the second definition of dedicated (enthusiastic), maybe our relationships might flourish.

Deployments dragged a soldier's mind on a wide range of meanderings. Eventually, I came across the right answer when I thought about a problem long enough. My issue was turning solutions into action. With the divorce rate at fifty percent, and seemingly higher in the military, many soldiers struggled to maintain happy marriages, myself included. Distance always made hearts grow fonder. I think some soldiers assessed whether or not they were in a stable relationship based on whether their wives or girlfriends stuck around after the deployment. When I returned home, I wanted to follow through with that sentiment of loving more compellingly.

Missing home wasn't always sunshine. Sometimes the problems back home filtered into combat. One day when I called home Tia was upset about a sergeant major who came into the mess hall and scolded a private for not yelling "at ease" when he entered. She defended the private and the sergeant major entered a staring contest with her, which she obliged. I absorbed it and voiced my opinion. She quickly dismissed my sentiment that the private needed to defend himself. Her motherly instincts wouldn't allow that notion to manifest and she slammed the phone down on the receiver.

For some reason, I felt some of my hearing loss occurred from that. "Wow," was all I could manage to mumble, counting the concentric holes on the phone's earpiece. Moments like that, I wrote.

When life got stressful, I retreated to pen and paper. Pen and paper allowed me to become a general. A sound tactician, battling my fears, expounding hopes and avoiding suicidal notes. To hell with disrespectful sergeant majors and misguided generals.

I understood Tia's anger. I lived it every day. I dealt with disrespect from master sergeants to lieutenant colonels. There wasn't a civilian sticking up for me.

My dad's voice echoed, *Don't let anyone disrespect you!* Hopefully, the private figured it out.

When my wife slammed the phone, all I could do was grin. Life would offer more bullshit tomorrow. More houses and IEDs would detonate. More privates would fail to yell "at ease." Shit happened repeatedly, so I couldn't get caught up in emotions.

Learn to let go. Learn to forgive. In the past, I would have probably called her back and hung up on her. The past few days had given me much to think about. Soldiers were starting to sustain injuries. What if I called her back and acted in kind? Karma might've had the last word. At any time, I could have an IED waiting on me. Her last memory couldn't be of me acting in kind. Some random soldier clipping my name from the *Army Times* and Tia being the only one knowing how petty I had been by calling and hanging up.

I hoped the recently injured soldiers dealt with missing home in a mature way. We were blinded by so much trivial shit that we overlooked important stuff. I ended the day sending her an email. Hopefully, it soothed whatever hurt she felt. And I prayed the rest of my buddies acted likewise.

The hell I hoped to avoid by not coming to Iraq searched for a fissure in my belief system. The devil grabbed a zippered volcano's pull-tab and began pulling. He was determined to undress all the ugliness war had to offer. And I was positioned where I could not look away.

LEARNING CURVES

~September 11, 2007~

A day America would never forget was an untrue statement. For some, 2001 was already a lifetime ago. The world moved quickly, jumping from one tragedy to the next: attacks in Paris, vehicles weaponized against pedestrians, or pick any mass shooting. It all added to our amnesia. Even so, details were worth remembering.

September 11 was already being inserted into school history books. It would soon be a footnote in newer editions. Would students born after 2010 learn why we invaded Iraq? Would they discuss Islam, Sunnis, Kurds, Shiites, or the Taliban? Would they learn of the quagmire of U.S. politics? Or the economic effects of the longest war in U.S. history?

A few years ago, in August 2015, Marcy Borders, a survivor of the 9/11 attacks, died of stomach cancer. On September 11, 2007, her story was on TV in the mess hall. Her picture became iconic when she emerged from the rubble covered in dust, her mouth somewhat clean as she shielded it to aid her breathing. Her lungs revolted against polluted air. In a few years, the world won't care about the war or her passing. I wondered how long it would take for us to become history's footnotes.

Ironic that we officially took over our AO when patrols intensified after 9/11 and before Ramadan (September 14). We coordinated several patrols with Iraqi security forces (ISF) in preparation for the month-long religious event. Our focus was to train ISF to take on more responsibility.

I found it odd, during such a religious event, we needed to increase patrols. Religion made god an anomaly. It disconnected us from spirituality and what we ought to be. It made us more foe than friend and stifled forward thinking. Iraq was a place where people prayed every morning and evening, and blood was shed at the end of every amen.

One thing about war, it was decent money. I amassed $1,900 in checking in a relatively short time. A lot of soldiers returned home and discarded perfectly good televisions for newer ones five inches larger. That too was maddening; destruction, religion, and waste ran hand and hand.

One of our first solo missions was a night operation with the Iraqi Army. Maybe it was Ramadan or another religious reason, but walking through the northern section of our area felt Babylonian. I MapQuested the Tower of Babel and its remnants were nearby.

The neighborhood we patrolled was ancient with cobbled alleyways. Its streets were so tight a small car might have gotten wedged between buildings. Buildings were comprised of mud. Long curtains hung to keep prying eyes from looking in. Residents kept their doors open to aid air circulation. Every house radiated with a candle glow of electricity when the curtains wafted.

That portion of our sector was closest to the river. At the COP, we might have been hit by sniper fire if we ventured close to the riverbank, but this area allowed us to be feet away because the houses provided cover.

The river was a natural barrier from the earth-denting detonations we heard in 3rd Squadron's battlespace. Around a corner, two old men played checkers as young gents awaited their turn. It was quite an experience to see something different besides the back of my truck. Alpha Section guarded vehicles for a change while Bravo dismounted.

When we mounted the truck, Sanchy spoke over the intercom to Stanley. Sanchy regaled him with how he met Mrs. Sanchez, no doubt a conversation they had been discussing while walking the neighborhood. Sergeant Nelly chimed in about his most drunken moment.

Of course, Nelly's story was the best laugh until I told them how I'd hung spread-eagle on the Fort Knox gold repository fence. It didn't hurt to embellish a little. We made it back in time so the guys could make late-night chow, while the lieutenant and I conducted a mission debrief.

Lieutenant Drexler earned his paycheck as we learned on a curve. During one of our routine checks of the hospital, we found that the adjacent neighborhood had spliced into the hospital's generator. Drexler directed the Iraqi Army to cut the splice. Of course, the neighborhood was outraged and Drexler conveniently pointed his finger at the Iraqi lieutenant, who in turn pointed his finger back at Drexler. It was classic bureaucracy in action.

We took negotiation classes prior to deploying to avoid those types of situations. Novio advised against cutting the splice because it would create another problem without a viable solution. At that time, the LT's decision made sense, but Novio's insight aligned with Negotiation 101. Pissing the Iraqi people off turned them into potential combatants.

We forced our rights on people who had no problem pointing out our wrongs. Through our eyes, no matter how small the infraction, the splice represented corruption.

One of the lieutenant's tasks was to restrict cash flow into black-market channels. The gas station was notorious for overcharging citizens in order to fund nefarious activities. The splice represented bleed-over. Because the whole country was corrupt, its citizens must've been too.

My inclination was that our dollars were being siphoned into terrorist's hands. All the money we spent on the FOB—what prevented it from flowing into the wrong hands?

Several of our officers were convicted of taking kickbacks from projects around Iraq. Millions of tax dollars flowed through Iraq daily. If money bred corruption in honest men, what other scandals awaited discovery?

Instead of cutting the wire, why couldn't we provide another generator? War's give and take were indistinguishable. Ultimatums and lines drawn were how armies operated. One maintained control by forcing the other to relinquish the stick's short end.

Cutting the wire was the easiest solution to a complex problem. It was a dictatorial fix. And as America could attest, when people lived without for too long, resentment worsened. As much as Iraqis appreciated Saddam's eradication, they despised us too. We may have been more lenient, accommodating, and a universe removed from Saddam's brutality, but we wielded the key to economic chains and were accustomed to profiting from bondage.

Had Iraq functioned better under dictatorial rule? I made the argument that slavery was America's tyrannical system. And it was, at least economically and somewhat socially. Perhaps Iraqis felt like the freed slaves during America's reconstruction period. Blacks observed whites' upward mobility while whites politized issues that anchored blacks to the sea floor. Our government reallocated monies forcing the impoverished toward deeper poverty.

Was this neighborhood a microcosm of American history? The Iraqis witnessed hospital lights bright while living by candlelight. As soldiers, we couldn't allow the hospital to fail even if we empathized with their plight. Alas, no one shared power amicably; therefore, dictatorship necessitated who received the stick's short end.

The morning following our riverbank mission, we were tasked to clear a high-rise building on Haifa Street. Red-One used one section. I suggested we take three trucks instead of four so we could add more men to Alpha's dismount team and leapfrog floors. Technically, it should have been a troop-size mission. Twelve guys, sixteen floors, numerous rooms, sweat, and heat wearing back-breaking gear. Alpha Section was spent, which intensified Red-Two's memory of the wire-cutting incident.

When I was a drill sergeant, Command Sergeant Major Burns said, "Let lieutenants make mistakes. It's how they learn."

Drexler learned, and while he and Alpha learned, the rest of us secured ground level. The problem was, if Bravo was fatigued waiting at ground level, imagine what curse words Novio mumbled by the ninth floor. I wondered if Burns was correct? If a general, who was once a lieutenant, made the same historical mistakes as the last general, who was also once a lieutenant, what was being learned? Sometimes discomfort caused us to miss the most essential blessing: everyone returned to base safely.

The past couple of days had made the nuances of war officially mundane and pointless. We drove in the wee hours of night asking Iraqi checkpoints what their needs were. They all said the same thing: "Nothing."

Augustus insisted we go. He called it our assessment phase. It made no sense assessing what we already knew for the possibility of an attack.

At one particular traffic-control point, Red-One had a chance to teach some Iraqi police a few curse words using our interpreter while he passed out cancer sticks.

"Hey LT, we should get moving," I nudged him.

Sitting in one spot too long brought about an uneasiness. Too many stories about one of our supposed allies going rogue for jihad.

The security forces compound was outside of the city, so Iraq's lights could not hinder God's brilliance that hung above us at night. I looked up as Drexler finished coordinating for a follow-on mission and I was reduced to my smallest element. We were nothing more than fleeting thoughts, bouncing from one neuron to the next. We could not make a ripple in the ocean, let alone the universe. And our universe was vast, and still, it was nothing more than a grain of sand on a beach, and beyond that, it extended for infinity.

Scientists believe trillions of stars have existed, which proves sight doesn't aid in our comprehension. If I had guessed a million, I would have been billions off, and I was only seeing a quarter of the hemisphere's sky. A faithful breeze carried the acoustics of a cricket symphony, focusing my attention on the dangers of here and now versus there and then. Gunfire crackled across the river; I was glad to be where I was, but wished to be even further removed from wondering which security personnel could be trusted.

My high school principal would pray we found favor among men. My high school friends had successful careers: educators, doctors, lawyers, and business owners, among other high achievers. I was a soldier. I envied their career paths. I didn't believe any of them would trade places with me. I'd definitely trade them. They completed four years of college or more and were settled, climbing the staircase of success. But the thing was, I wouldn't trade if it meant them having to be where I was. I would not want anyone I cared about to endure that. Iraq made me aware of selfless acts. If the nation must wage an unnecessary war, let it be me and not them who went.

Sometimes the night sky amplified not only how small we were, but how grand sacrifice could be.

The following morning, the sun and sand particles filtered in an orange haze. The haze meant visibility was low, and that grounded air assets. We were on QRF, which meant if anyone was attacked, they would not be able to call for a MEDDEVAC, which increased the likelihood they'd need our assistance. As the morning evaporated, so did the haze.

The air-conditioning stopped working so most of us opted to hang out in the motor pool. Alpha Section soldiers complained to Top, aka first sergeant, about Novio, and Top asked me to address the issue. Initially, I thought they were just bitching, as most soldiers did. "Why do we need to wear kneepads?" and "Why do we have to do physical fitness on our refit days?" were frequent complaints.

Their concerns were merited. Novio's corrective training rarely fit the infraction. He used a bazooka when a flyswatter would suffice. For instance, he wanted to punish Whitey for being late and was going to make him pull guard duty for the twelve hours. I intervened on Whitey's behalf. Novio had been calibrated from his first deployment. He lost a few guys and didn't want to lose any more.

With command influence pressuring Drexler, he reluctantly counseled Novio, Pope, and me when my plan wasn't effective.

"The next time I hear you call a soldier anything other than his name, dire repercussions will follow," he told Novio in between Alpha Section's trucks.

We recognized his idle threat as such, but he sold it well. Novio loved to call his soldiers "fuck-face." That didn't bother them as much as the bullshit he had them doing after the term of endearment.

Drexler told me to keep my head in the game. He could tell my focus had shifted. Once the command sergeant major told me he was moving me, I had to balance being there with knowing I wasn't going to be there. Pope was directed to loosen the reins in order to maximize time.

After our counseling, we discussed our concerns with the junior NCOs. They came to a consensus that the section sergeants needed to back off and let them step up. We dropped a few tasks, but it was necessary for everyone's development. Case in point: Novio told Demerit to gather some cables, antennas, and a few other gadgets to improve Alpha's radios. Demerit used his memory instead of note-taking skills and forgot some items. Novio called him "fuck-face" under his breath.

~September 19, 2007~

Third Squadron lost its first soldier. The elusive sniper finally hit his mark. Sniper fire for 3rd Squadron was a run-of-the-mill occurrence, like car accidents back in the states. Unbelievable events became part of their normal routine. We knew danger existed, but we never comprehended it happening until it did. In the states, one could opt out of riding in a car after an accident, but in Iraq, we couldn't negate fear by using avoidance. After we heard about the sniper actually killing a soldier, we sunk lower in our hatches as we rode around to make ourselves harder targets.

The chain of command followed strict protocol and severed communications until the soldier's family was notified. It was a mind game for our loved ones. They knew when we couldn't call that something terrible had happened. Word spread quickly and the spouses usually heard what happened before we did.

While 3rd Squadron was in the thick of it, we eased our way into the fray. My first hair-raising incident occurred near the imam's house. A car barreled toward us while we were dismounted. D-Nasty, our dismount team leader, fired a non-lethal shotgun round, shattering the windshield as the driver screeched to a halt. Our muscle memory worked. Another few feet and my thumb would have flipped the safety and my bullets would have been added to his nonlethal round. For once, I was glad for a younger man's video-game reflexes.

The kids who surrounded us made it eerier. They begged and tugged on our pants for attention. Instinctively, I distanced myself from them, nearly tripping over the curb trying to create a better shooting angle. My thumb never ventured from the weapon's safety.

The next morning, we showed VIPs and Colonel Augustus's personal security detail around our AO. Sabre Six Delta (driver) rear-ended my Stryker twice. It was confirmation our area wasn't large enough for two units. During the second fender bender, Sergeant Major Lowery reiterated that he wasn't pulling me until February.

I suggested he reconsider. Now was the perfect time for a new guy to get acclimated. I was always cognizant of the first thirty days and the last thirty days. February held too many unknowns.

Top was there for the dog-and-pony show and made an offhand comment, "Don't start looking for another job yet."

It was funny because I had a sense he'd wanted my unorthodox ass gone since Fort Lewis. When I first took over the platoon, Top said I wouldn't have to do much to stand out in squadron. I told him I'd rather be the worst person in the best organization than the best person in the worst organization. Difference of perspective was why I never meshed well with him.

My gut feeling was my whole platoon would be different. Either Novio or Pope would be moved to 3rd Platoon and Drexler was on tap to be Pale Horse Troop's executive officer (XO). Hopefully, the troop would achieve the balance he sought.

If there was a reason to stay with my boys, I felt I could protect them from bullshit. Drexler had confided that headquarters was planning to send us on an air assault mission in Taji. Taji was part of the Sunni Triangle, one of the most dangerous areas in all of Iraq. "Are you crazy sir? We have three guys air-assault qualified. Most of us would have trouble tying fishing knots. Why in the world would they wait until we are in combat to have us do something we aren't qualified for?" I bitched, releasing tension gathering in my wrist.

He was only the messenger. Fast-roping from a helicopter sounded fun from a movie theater chair, not so much in Iraq. I would have bet money it was Augustus's idea, and he came up with it while smoking hash during downtime.

We returned to the FOB and the sergeant major came over as we were locking our vehicles and said he wanted me to get a couple more months of combat-rated time. Glad he took time to explain it. Squadron might not be bad.

While stowing equipment, Krafty, one of Red-Two's dismounts, hit himself in the eye with a bungee cord. Red-Two and my crew loaded back up and took him to the CASH. Doc said a centimeter over, and he would have to go to Landstuhl hospital.

His luck reminded me that we had a lucky charm hidden somewhere. I think it was due to a private I had from basic training who transferred to us back in Germany from headquarters section. He was infamous for creating the Cobra Canteen. Cobras was our platoon name in basic training. He was above average in height, hairy to the point that his back and neck hairs poked from his T-shirt neckline, and he wore trifocals, so he appeared as if he were conducting experiments to shrink someone's kids.

The story went that he placed the tip of his dick on a buddy's canteen and deposited vegetable growth serum in it. Once I heard that, I told him he could drink his own radioactive material or try someone else's. He chose his own glow-in-the-dark substance. Thus, a tradition was born. Any soldier after that cycle who failed to exhibit proper battle-buddy standards had to drink from that canteen. Of course, it had been sterilized and the backstory wasn't revealed until after the troublesome soldier drank from it.

In Germany, Cobra Canteen Creator put his boots on the wrong feet. Novio pointed it out to me after the sergeant major had us fall out of formation so we could hear the commander better. Cobra Canteen Creator had his legs crossed to make it seem as if his boots were on correctly. I hadn't seen anything funnier that had me so irate. I told him to go behind the vehicles and fix it before he embarrassed the platoon.

He had to be why we were lucky. Whether we went to the Sunni Triangle or not, God, luck, something other than our training would go with us. Gomer Pyle, Forrest Gump, and Cobra Canteen Creator-type characters were impervious to harm.

~September 27, 2007~

Sergeant First Class Randy Johnson from 2nd Squadron was killed by an IED. He is survived by his wife and two sons. They lived next door to Noriega's family, a few houses from mine. Tia said Deuce ran into the house hysterical when a black sedan turned our corner. Deuce assumed the sedan was coming to our house. We did all that preparation and forgot to cover casualty notification with our kids. War had hit close to home, and the hopelessness I felt manifested in their helplessness.

Vilseck was home. It had rolling green hills and cobblestone streets. It was a community that didn't seem to need mortuary affair officers. It didn't need apologies such as, "Ma'am, I'm sorry to inform you that your soldier was killed in action for the service of his country." Germany had done a wonderful job hiding her World War scars. Mrs. Johnson did not need new wounds added to old. Regrettably, those notifications came more frequently.

I wanted to lash out but there was nowhere to direct my fury. It was bullshit. Saudi Arabian citizens and the Taliban in Afghanistan were responsible for 9/11. Iraq had nothing do it with it. Already, Johnson, Perez, Walker, and Randall had been killed. Their names were added to a growing tally. I couldn't reconcile why America sent us. Johnson's father said his son felt the same.

While researching, I found an NBC News article by Tracy Connor from May 21, 2015, that stated a British cab driver named Anis Sardar was convicted in London for Randy's murder. According to the FBI's Terrorist Explosive Device Analytical Center database, Sardar's fingerprints were found on IED debris and later linked to a bomb-making cell from Syria. Some of Randy's men were in disbelief that someone was actually convicted.

"I hope they nail his ass to the wall and burn the wall down," Luke Stinson said during an interview. Luke tried to save Sergeant First Class Johnson's life. Johnson was incapacitated after the IED ripped into his Stryker. One soldier's leg was severely injured, but Johnson absorbed the brunt of it. Randy woke up suddenly and grabbed Luke tightly. "Don't let me die," was Johnson's final request. The medic tried to insert an intravenous syringe into Randy's flattened veins. The enemy chose to target the platoon sergeant's truck instead of the first, second, or third.

God had gotten lost in the middle of Iraq. I wanted to believe there was a purpose for us being there, but every time a soldier died, I came face to face with an unanswerable "why."

"Lord, be a lamp unto our feet. Guide our path. Be my strong tower. Comfort Mrs. Johnson and her boys. Let the Vilseck community be strong," I prayed. I wanted to end my prayer with, "In all things give thanks."

Times such as those, Bible scriptures fell short. All I did was cry in the stillness of my tent. The air-conditioner whined, hiding my sobs. I wasn't supposed to grieve in a combat zone. Where could I have gone to hold a moment of silence when all I wanted to do was scream? Why did people speak as if there was ever a right time to speak again?

There would never be the right time because we kept adding new names to old. I kept asking why, and hated that I knew the answer.

The Iron Company infantry platoon attached to us was reassigned to 3rd Squadron in Sadr City. Their peaceful moment ended.

A day later, White-One (2nd platoon leader) informed us that two guys from Iron had been attacked. They had been with us at the COP two days before. They entered a booby-trapped house. One soldier lost a few fingers, possibly a hand. The other a leg, possibly his life. Had I written this journal with greater detail, I might have been able to recall a joke one of them told me, or what jar the other used to hold his tobacco spit, or the brand of cigarette filters muddled in the bottom of his spit container. Back then, I wanted to remain clueless. Now, I want to know everything. Shit escalated quickly.

A news correspondent said our death toll was the lowest it had been in fourteen months. It didn't seem that way when our buddies were tallied into it.

The zippered volcano the devil was undressing spewed lava as the roller coaster I didn't want to be on was far from ending. The rest of my time in Iraq left me wishing I could go back in time and forgo ever earning a combat patch.

My time with Outlaw Red would end in three days. The sergeant major thought it best to make the move sooner than later. Top moved Krafty, Billy Badass, and Pope to 3rd Platoon and I received two of their sergeants. Pope took the move hard. Top wanted to balance the platoons. Second Platoon already functioned to his liking.

My last mission with Outlaw Troop occurred roughly two months after my arrival. I was supposed to call my daughter, but a time-sensitive mission took priority. When we got the call to get ready, I wanted to vomit. The coward in me sunk ankle-low and tied weights to my feet. Sluggishly, I acted unafraid. It was the last time my soldiers would need me. Once the mission was over, I could stop pretending to be the Rock of Gibraltar when I felt like a pebble.

We received intel that a high-value target's cell phone pinged near his house. An informant corroborated the information. During the mission brief, we experienced difficulty deciphering whether the informant was trustworthy.

The target was an Iraqi general allegedly working with al-Qaeda. We went to his house. He wasn't there. We received word he was at a pool hall. That information was false. Would the next intel lead us to an IED? Every location seemed a ruse. *Would the next spot be it?* I thought.

The devil didn't need help coloring night dark to keep secrets hidden. He undressed our wrongs right in front of our eyes. Closing our eyes would not mute screams. Covering our ears didn't eliminate the stench. All humans suffered from the same affliction. The person who provided the intel was probably caught in a moral dilemma. Not speaking up may have kept him alive that day, but karma never closed her eyes. It was my turn to blindly follow orders from one dangerous spot to the next.

I remembered touring Dachau concentration camp. The German citizens living there battled that kind of duplicity. The smoke from the crematory encircled the city's perimeter, and the smell of burning flesh eventually perfumed fresh air to the point that gruesomeness became commonplace. They told themselves they needed to survive, so they minded their mouths and breathed the air with broken inhalations. And that first step toward self-preservation and silence started their souls sliding. One thing was certain: war exposed the worst in us.

The enemy increased its use of house-borne IEDs. I prayed for 3rd Squadron because they were getting hit hard. Whatever initiative we had when the war started had been lost entering houses and hoping they didn't explode.

Further intel reported the Iraqi police had alerted the general as soon as we left the FOB. So, the people we worked with worked against us. It was a perilous game we played. Luckily, the general was focused on evading instead of killing, because his house could have easily been rigged to kill.

That day, I saw what policing the world looked like and why Vietnam had failed. Also, why the Bay of Pigs was an erroneous endeavor, and why dethroning a dictator was a waste of time. Policing the world was not our birthright. We continued to view other countries' problems through a faulty foreign-affairs lens.

The minute we found out the police had warned the general, we should have packed our bags and never returned. But we drudged through bullshit hoping to find a finish line of bliss. My last mission with Outlaw taught me it was no use protecting a perimeter with a rotten center.

We gambled, and everyone returned to base alive. I hated that I wasn't able to call my daughter. It seemed world affairs took precedence over more important matters. That was my lesson learned.

Red-Four signing off.

Lewis on a street adjacent to an Iraqi hospital

TACTICAL OPERATIONS CENTER

~November 1, 2007~

My first day working at S-3 (Squadron Operations and Planning Section), I became a Fobbit. Fobbits were personnel who never left a FOB.

The tactical operations center (TOC) was headquartered in what was once Saddam's pool house. The pool was roughly 100 meters away and was one of the few masonry structures besides the palace. Most of the buildings consisted of aluminum sheds or double-wide trailers. Inside the TOC, we had makeshift plywood workstations. It was a U-shaped design with an intel guy and an air force targeting expert to my left. My computer was center, and controlled the huge screen we looked at every night. The battle captain sat behind me at a folding table with several telephones. A slew of equipment blocked the right side, limiting access to all the wires crisscrossing the floor.

On eventful nights, we watched unmanned aerial vehicle (UAV) video feeds of platoons conducting house-to-house searches. I provided a play-by-play for the other Fobbits. When we didn't have UAV, the blaring generator outside competed with an electronic black box that hummed inside, leading to boring evenings.

The duty was easy and less stressful than being out in sector. Keeping the coffee hot, which I failed at intentionally, and maintaining the generator were my main tasks. All the sections—S-1 (personnel); S-2 (intel) and S-6 (communications)—depended on S-3 to function; therefore, we were the point of deconfliction. In addition, I recorded and consolidated patrol reports, built and deconflicted patrol schedules, and coordinated patrol requests.

For instance, Pale Horse Troop reported finding several cache sites. Outlaw reported finding a rudimentary bomb maker who made a mistake and painted his walls with himself. Outlaw Six and his Mortar Platoon supervised cleanup on aisle bombmaking-gone-wrong. Nemesis Troop reported capturing a military-age male posing as an Iraqi soldier. Nemesis found him tucked away in a sniper position. I rolled up their reports so the battle captain could update Augustus and our operations major in the morning.

On paper, we did our part in the war on terror. Constantly finding caches reminded me of an Armed Forces Network commercial about depression. A man was at a beach digging a hole against the tide and it kept refilling with sand. The advertisement went on to ask, "Doesn't this seem like a hopeless endeavor?"

First Cavalry Division returned in 2009. They served as our divisional leadership and would undoubtedly discover more cache sites on their fourth or fifth tour. I had lost count. Continually finding caches was like the man digging while the sand kept shifting. The tide of caches would never cease.

One thing I learned fairly quickly was that one simple reporting error created legal loopholes bad guys slipped through. Patrols had to take pictures of evidence and maintain impeccable chain-of-custody standards to make war crimes stick. Strange calling it a war crime when we invaded them. We had forty-eight hours to fix reporting discrepancies before brigade pressed S-2 for information. Squadron was just another spoke in an already congested hamster's wheel, and no matter where I was, I spun in it.

I performed a few days working at the TOC then rotated to the COP for a few days. The operations sergeant major had me monitoring radios on twelve-hour shifts for two days. It was a last-minute mission, so I forgot to pack shower shoes and dreaded the single-celled organisms that propagated in the showers. If a small IED attack only flattened a tire, I would have rather endured it than step into those showers. I wrapped garbage bags around my feet and lived dangerously.

After surviving bio contamination, I began my shift. One of the infantrymen who'd encountered a house-borne IED days before was on shift. He was sent back to us because he suffered from PTSD. I read the article about the attack. Two were KIA, another's leg had been severed, and another remained in critical condition. Hence, White-One's initial report was inaccurate, and the correct version sanitized it. The reporters didn't give details that mattered. Was his leg dismembered at the knee or hip? It mattered during recovery.

During the three weeks that followed, 3rd Squadron encountered three IEDs. It was hard to believe I was exposed to those kinds of dangers days before. As the surviving infantryman sat near a stack of radios and reflected on what happened, his pupils widened. His voice labored as he wiped away a tear with his sleeve. He placed the hand mic on the table as if he needed a break from being a soldier. The white tile and fluorescent lights were in direct contrast to the gloom that exited his vocal cords. I sat on the edge of a folding chair listening.

The article stated the stairwell was rigged with a 120 mm artillery round. It praised our inceptor body armor (IBA) vests for saving lives. Explosions ripped away everything not covered by it. One's torso was good; everything else was obliterated.

One of the problems with our protective gear was its effectiveness. It was problematic because it created new diagnoses that should not have existed. An explosion that produced instantaneous Alzheimer's symptoms usually killed us. Now, it didn't. Soldiers forgot three-item grocery lists. Or lacked a desire to read because a joyful thing had become painful. Surviving had a price.

The soldier's command team boasted they were the "tip of the spear" when they arrived. The infantryman would not say it, it was against a warrior's better nature to admit it, but he may have felt relieved to be back on our side of the river. Leaders had to buy into military slogans they didn't necessarily believe. "The tip of the spear" was one of those statements.

"Burnt flesh was something you never forget after seeing and smelling it," he said, sinking lower than before.

I wanted to take some of the weight off him. I felt as helpless as I did back at Fort Knox listening to returning veterans talk about their combat experiences. A chasm was between him and me. As he slipped deeper into his crevice, his eyes grew distant. I extended my hand imaginarily as if I could pull him back to solid ground. "It's going to be OK," was all I could say.

I didn't know this fact then, but some soldiers who smelled burning flesh hate going to barbecues or camping because the smell of charcoal transports them back to a horrific event. Even the stench of garbage triggers unwanted visions or, worse yet, anger, fear, regret, or resentment.

My shower shoe gripe made me feel infinitesimal. Third Squadron fought for survival. The tip of the spear was bent, and they kept stabbing with it.

It took a rocket propelled grenade (RPG) landing in the outpost parking lot to bring us out of his darkened reverie. War was like that; danger had a way of making things seem better. Even though the RPG was a dud, our side of the river grew more ominous.

My first fixable incident occurred the second day at the COP. Supply requests were color-coded. Green equaled good; yellow meant we used a little; red meant critical; and black meant empty.

We came close to losing power because resupply didn't account for refueling the generators. Lieutenant Baron said the Iraqis stole some fuel. The real problem was Baron's recollection. I told Baron that Sergeant First Class Connell reported we were red on fuel, but the lieutenant disregarded the information. When the generator sputtered, he wanted to blame Iraqis. He should have requested fuel during the last log-stat report.

In addition to fuel running low, we ran out of hot chow. Luckily, we had Meals Ready-to-Eat, which had expiration dates that read like a *Star Trek* captain's log. War became a reporting drill.

Upon leaving the outpost, I told a soldier from 3rd Platoon to correct his uniform.

"We only do that when the first sergeant comes around," he said, ending his statement by saying his platoon sergeant told him it was OK. That's why Top transferred Pope.

Pope was still bummed dealing with the shenanigans of 3rd Herd. They reveled in kicking in doors and slapping the natives around. Pope was smart enough to know that behavior came at a cost. It was chaos versus order, creating resentment versus winning hearts and minds.

I told him, "Never get so focused on one thing that you lose sight of everything."

Back at the base, I linked up with him again in line at the mess hall. He was a by-the-book leader and was ostracized because of it. He revealed an incident that occurred after his transfer.

Third Herd entered the FOB yelling profanities at an Iraqi guard. The sentinel flipped the soldiers off, and later that evening a couple of soldiers, two NCOs with their interpreter, went back to the gate and roughed up the guard. All the brawlers received punishment and were demoted. Platoon leadership was baffled that it had happened, but bullshit begot bullshit.

Pope also mentioned they shot Iraqis with paintballs for the heck of it and shot down kites. It was believed insurgents used kites for signaling our presence. I understood kites. Shooting people was over the top. When people grew tired of killing scrawny dogs, paint balls were the next step up. Thank god we weren't in Vietnam. They might have been the ones indicted for village massacres.

Besides Pope's blues, Outlaw Red adjusted to my departure well. Pale Horse White-Four, aka Noriega, landed in trouble. His section sergeants accused him of pointing his weapon at soldiers in a threatening manner, shooting vehicles without reporting it, and stealing a car from his sector for personal use on the FOB.

The good part about working at the TOC was that I heard the truth before it changed into a rumor. When leadership questioned him, the rumor was, he blackmailed the commander, who allegedly had an illegal AK-47. Noriega used the monkey see, monkey do defense, and it worked.

His platoon kicked ass, but at what cost? He had deployed during the initial invasion of Iraq, and operated with a *Rambo* mindset. Unfortunately, that mindset wasn't what the generals needed. His platoon captured a couple of high-value targets and found the largest weapons cache.

Noriega claimed his section sergeants stole valuables during raids. That's what happened when the ship started sinking—every man had water to sell. The command covered their asses and Noriega followed the army promotion pattern of mess up, move up.

By the time we returned to Germany, he'd made E-8. A few years later, he attended the Sergeants Major

Academy at Fort Bliss. Squadron needed more like him. Waging war required a certain demented mentality, to get results anyway. I could have learned a lot from him, if I wasn't so dead-set on avoiding bullshit altogether.

Upon returning to my containerized housing unit, the thermometer dangling on its awning read 172 degrees. It had to have been broken. The devil walked around in his drawers and fanned himself like an elderly church lady wearing a gigantic Easter hat. I couldn't speak Arabic, but I imagined the Iraqis said, *oh child, it's hot as shit out here.*

The following day, heading to the mess hall before shift, I ran into a private from basic training. He graduated from my last class. He said Sergeant Maurer was his section sergeant. Maurer had graduated my original class. It displayed how quickly scouts were thrust into leadership roles. The private said he would tell Maurer I looked happy. An odd observation, considering where we were. I must have really personified El Diablo to them. I was glad they watched each other's backs.

That night, Iron Company's 1st Platoon encountered a house-borne IED. A soldier lost a leg at the knee and two others suffered traumatic brain injuries (TBI).

Two days later, Iron's 2nd Platoon encountered an IED while convoying on Route Senators. Route Senators was a major highway that led north from Baghdad International Airport. It had been treacherous for convoys for a year and was called IED alley. If one could avoid travelling on it, it was favorable to do that. Platoons were guaranteed to develop a TBI diagnosis on it.

I imagined how a lieutenant rationalized traveling on it. I'd rather affix wings to a Stryker and fly over it than drive it. That was the sad irony of being a leader. Even though we wanted to voice our objections, we kept quiet and executed our mission.

With so many attacks happening, I wondered if the conscientious objector had been right? Was I complicit? Was I marching to the tune of "Whistling Dixie," heading toward misdirection? Had we gone so far down the wrong path that we viewed what we were doing as right? Everything about Iraq was wrong. America's decision to invade Iraq created a gigantic pile of crap a lieutenant had to shovel on his platoon. Route Senators was where corrupt and wrong collided.

While Iron Company soldiers were losing their limbs and memories, I iced my back after playing in a basketball game. Sergeant Major Lowery talked with the most severely injured and said he was in good spirits.

Consequently, the newspaper clippings lessened due to cooler weather. Desert people didn't like fighting in the cold. Unfortunately, winter wouldn't last long. I'd be back to feeling guilty taking jump shots, while others struggled to walk. Spring meant attacks would increase, which was incongruous with the natural order of life.

I came across this statement while researching. *The Dao that could be told was not the eternal Dao.* It was a simple statement that dismantled every religious construct I had been taught. I would need something redefining for what lay ahead.

Right outside the gate, at Entry Control Point (ECP) 2, Pale Horse Troop received their first KIA. We detained and questioned the Iraqi police because the IED was placed in full view of their position. Dastardly! No number of motherfuckers or goddamns came close to the words we wanted to say to the bastards responsible for security.

It was as if they conducted a physics experiment. The gate was a cage. The bomb was a variable, and we were its test subjects. I wanted to believe they had fallen asleep, but I knew that wasn't the case. They knew an American had a date with death and gave no warning. It should never be easy watching someone's demise. We made it easy for them to make us martyrs.

We searched the guards' houses for intel. For all the guys wanting to deploy, there it was. The ugly immoral truth. A truth that resided within a lie; and it needed to be confronted, even though I wanted nothing to do with it. It tapped my shoulder in the quiet of night and asked, *Was this what y'all came for?* America's lie made me feel dark inside.

It was grotesque and unforgiveable. Unwinnable. Lieutenant Peter Burks shouldn't have died like that. Five of his soldiers had been injured. Before he died, he was able to ask if his guys were OK.

Every time I exited ECP 2, I was reminded of the political lie that made truth a dirty word. I reconciled truth by reminding myself our presence in Iraq kept darkness from creeping toward America.

Maybe that was purpose enough, but what happens if we become that darkness?

The next few days we weren't allowed to talk to our loved ones because Peter's parents had to be notified. Their fear materialized as ours disintegrated into unchecked hatred. Losing Peter Burks was like watching light disappear from the cosmos. Another newspaper clipping to be added to this book. The bravest among us would never be able to love, toss the child he hoped for in the air, or embrace his fianceé.

To die without rendering a kiss goodbye was war's regret. Pale Horse 4th Platoon was Specialist Burkhart's unit. Today was the worst day yet. November 14, 2007. Rest in heaven, Peter.

I brought my journal to the TOC; all I wanted to do was write. A few days had passed without an entry. After reading 2 Kings I fashioned an idea. The amount of one's knowledge was a reflection of the success one had. King Solomon was my favorite Bible character. Proverbs was as far as I got before I lost interest in reading the Bible in its entirety. I questioned its validity compared to the Koran. Which one was right?

Follow me, not them. He did it right. They did it wrong. Your path leads to hell. His to heaven. Hell existed here. I no longer believed it existed elsewhere. Heaven existed as glimpses trapped in simple desires absorbed on my face like rays of sunshine on wintry days. Heaven faded away every day. Heaven had to exist beyond a place for eternal worship. God's written word in man's penmanship was what I questioned.

War in this region hinged on a religious divide widened by corporate greed. Remove religion, and I wondered if there would be war at all. We waged war using different arms of the same god. It reminded me of the Hindu goddess Durga, stabbing herself with her eight arms. My thoughts took me back to what had happened a few days before. A heaviness hovered over my unit. People moped instead of marched. Enthusiasm was gone. Anger built like an electric charge waiting for a conduit.

Fighting, as we knew it, changed. We wanted to go toe-to-toe but couldn't. Fighting an insurgency wasn't a tit-for-tat affair. We've always been plagued with that revolutionary mindset. We constantly added rules to warfare. Too much bloodshed made hardened warriors harder. We added rules in an attempt to keep our souls honest. We thought we could protect ourselves from war's corruptibility.

We changed the second we stepped foot in Iraq. We were baptized in darkness. Surrounded by it. If truth did cover us, it had no redeeming qualities. When Peter was killed, I understood what combat meant. Whatever or whoever Dao was, I wished it could tell me: *what happened to the light?*

DIGITIZED WARFARE

"It is well that war is so terrible, otherwise we should grow too fond of it." —*Robert E. Lee*

~December 8, 2007~

Squadron didn't expect so many staff sergeants to make the promotion list. In order to make room for newly promoted platoon sergeants, I volunteered to transfer to brigade as a liaison officer (LNO) at FOB Liberty. Captain Jefferies was my counterpart for the day shift. I worked from 2000-0800 hours.

Camp Liberty was situated near Baghdad International Airport (BIAP); therefore, the base was large enough to sustain the logistics of the second-largest city in the Arab world. FOB Prosperity's dimensions were prison-like compared to BIAP's size.

The FOB had a movie theater, library, USO (recreational chill spot), and swimming pool. It required a great deal of walking to get from place to place. Luckily, our sleeping quarters were near brigade headquarters.

LNO duty was routine. The battle captain tracked patrols and cleared fires (made sure friendlies weren't shooting at each other). Some places had daily contact (enemy attacks). Others had been quiet for months. Night shift consisted of consolidating squadron mission reports so Jefferies could brief in the morning. Unless we had troops in contact, there was no real requirement to deconflict anything. The real job was keeping squadron informed of targeting-meeting intel or give squadron a heads-up if the brigade commander was going to be in our AO. The work was hardly relevant to Iraq's success or failure.

Brigade TOC was larger than Squadron's and was set up in the same manner, except the brigade battle captain was centered in the room with about ten LNOs horseshoed around him. Whoever designed it must have been a Trekkie, because the battle captain was able push from his desk and swivel his command chair to see which one of us was expendable for miscellaneous errands.

The screen to everyone's front made the war a bloodless affair. This particular evening, we watched an infantry unit observing three insurgents emplacing an IED using aerial assets. The battle captain had the ability to tie into subordinate units' video feeds.

Choppers were dispatched. The insurgents heard rotary blades flapping in the distance and fled. One Hellfire missile zipped into the frame, and the screen flashed with a brilliant light. When the heat flash dissipated, filleted arms and legs rained toward earth. With one push of a trigger, IED diggers' blood muddied the sand.

A female officer went up to the screen and matched body parts to bodies. The footage was rewound several times to identify the missing leg. It reminded me of *Clear and Present Danger*. Cabinet members gathered around a screen sipping coffee, as if watching whole men turn into shards of matter was the thing to do before breakfast.

It was a win for us. It was one less IED we had to contend with. Still, it was unbelievable having a front-row seat to someone else's demise. The cheers made it more unsettling. I was juxtaposed in the sentinel's position when he watched Lieutenant Burks enter FOB Prosperity. Or the informant who laughed at us jumping from house to pool hall. Life was in freefall with one parachute for us all.

After about two months of working there, the TOC quieted around 0200 hours. I used the opportunity to go to the gym. When it calmed beyond that, I took power naps in my room. Twelve-hour shifts for seven days straight would be my routine until May. Time whizzed on as I balanced gym, work, and college classes. The job afforded me the opportunity to finish my last three classes for a bachelor's in business administration.

Sometimes I attended targeting meetings when my counterpart couldn't attend. There was a top-secret G-14 classified civilian who had been in Iraq since the war began. He had amassed a small fortune in contractor pay. He kept dossiers on top-level al-Qaeda operating in the brigade's footprint. He knew which politicians accepted bribes. Hell, his boss probably did the bribing. It was interesting to see the different levels of planning involved in war and shaping regime change at the local level.

The brigade commander had to support what was essentially the governor of our area. The classified civilian helped the colonel navigate political land mines. There was more to fighting a war than scouts kicking down doors.

The second week into work, we received word that Specialist Pickard shot himself in a Porta-John back at FOB Prosperity. It was probably the same Porta-John where the staff sergeant ended his career with Nanny McPhee. He belonged to 1st Cavalry out of Fort Hood, but I saw him at the dry cleaners a time or two. He should be remembered, regardless of how he died. In addition to all that we faced, soldiers combated their own demons, and the depression cycle ramped up as Christmas drew near.

Fortunately, regiment headquarters was at Liberty, and Chief Warrant Officer J-Crill was in charge of the regimental S-6 shop. He was a jovial dude, always chuckling. I would often go to him to remember better days. It was about a twenty-minute walk, so I used the opportunity to exercise and eat lunch with him before pretending to sleep in my room.

The year was almost over. Tia and Tasha, J-Crill's wife, had driven to Stuttgart to Christmas shop and almost had a life-altering accident. The autobahn forewent fender benders and went straight into trauma surgery territory. Luckily, a jerk of the steering wheel kept the paint intact as the tire treads thinned. I am certain Tia left out the details to ease my mind. I stayed focused on emergent issues and was glad when occurrences back home remained non-life threatening. I wanted to leave Iraq, but I didn't want to leave by having to visit Tia in the hospital.

My nephew, Jon-Jon, turned a year old on Christmas day. It was hard to believe I had a nephew I hadn't seen. Tia and the kids went to Garmisch and had a great time skiing. Diamond skied like Picabo Street. Deuce did as I had done the first time I skied in Colorado. He had his feet out in front of him and grabbed the skids with his hands and slid down the kiddie slope in four-point stance. Ryan grabbed a snowboard and graduated to an intermediate hill before lunch. Tia took photographs and wished I was there. I hoped it was the last holiday I spent away.

A few days into the new year, Tia informed me that Deuce got sloppy drunk. There was no way I could sleep after hearing that. She watched him the entire night to make sure he didn't choke to death. I visited J-Crill to vent.

Several missiles landed on the northern part of the FOB, which I heard about from Tia. They were still talking about it when I entered the TOC. Whenever counter-artillery was able to return fire, the night crew was more amped.

That evening, there was an unmanned aerial vehicle (UAV) video of several police officers beating an Iraqi man who had surrendered. They appeared to shoot into a crowd of people and the crowd dispersed quickly. Several civilians appeared to be hit. The battle major deemed the video detrimental to Iraq's national security and confiscated it. Everything was either geared toward bringing forth truth or suppressing it.

When days were especially boring, I chatted with the night battle captain. He was a midwesterner in his late twenties. His salt-and-pepper hair made him appear twenty years older.

He asked me how I managed to stay married so long being in the military.

I paused briefly. "Forgiveness. It's impossible to go through life without stepping on toes and doing wrong to someone. You can have the best of intentions and woefully miss the proverbial bull's eye. Forgiveness helps smooth the holes we dig ourselves in."

He went on to ask, "Is there such a thing as a perfect relationship?"

This was an odd question considering our audience, but the handful of LNOs that stuck around after all the important people left were bored also and eavesdropped.

"Many people regard Will and Jada Smith as having a perfect relationship. If there is one, it cannot be compared. Just because they fit, doesn't mean Sergeant Hughes would." I pointed to Hughes, who had been listening intently and shaking his head in disagreement.

"I'd fit just fine with Jada Pinkett," Hughes interjected.

"We do ourselves a disservice always searching for perfection. We'd be better off striving to limit the number of things we need to be forgiven for," I finished.

As an afterthought, someone else said, "That takes maturity."

My silence carried me further into my own cogitations. No one can fulfill all the needs of another. It would take two perfect people to make a perfect relationship. Therefore, perfection could never exist. Our imperfections, the way we matched strength with weakness, silence for outspokenness, love for shame, that was where our perfection lay.

My thoughts whisked me toward my father's presence in the home, and how not having his presence was similar to not knowing God's presence. I knew the uneasiness of not having my dad home. Would my sons feel my awkwardness as a father? Maybe it was this deployment weighing on me. Life, with its imperfections, was harder to live when God or a higher power was nowhere to be found. They say God was there in the midst of storms. War was the perfect storm to question life's existence.

A vaporization flashed across the video feed. A collective gasp escaped our throats as the battle captain's phone rang. Everyone snapped to attention and began coordinating with their respective units. The battle captain cleared airspace for a MEDEVAC. Reports later confirmed six killed and two wounded.

More newspaper clippings were added to my journal's pages. Generals said we progressed. Did company commanders feel the same? Was this the storm people spoke of? The operations center coordinated well into the morning. I left work wondering why man invented god when we tried our best to erase any evidence that he had ever existed within us.

There was talk of us returning in 2010. It was unconscionable to tell us we were returning while we were still there. I focused on R and R in five months. Regiment stated 4th Squadron would move to Baqubah after my R and R was over. I opted for the last slots so my soldiers could go. We would only have a few months left at that point.

Since I was raised near Atlanta, whenever I went home, I stayed at home and never took Tia anywhere. I had already seen what Atlanta had to offer. But she made sure we would not sit at home and do nothing. She planned on staying at a bed-and-breakfast and visiting the aquarium, the Coca-Cola museum, and Martin Luther King's birthplace.

Two days after the six KIA event, two IEDs took place in the same location a day apart. We reached an unachievable level of stupidity. Death was a constant reminder to enjoy life. Not the birthday present I wanted, but my dad called through Skype, and I did talk with Tia.

We lost another three soldiers the other day. One lost both legs. He came from 4th Infantry, Fort Hood, Texas. I hate to see what Iraq would become in twenty years.

As big as FOB Liberty was, the concertina surrounding it started shrinking. The prison feeling tightened as each day ticked. Scratch marks drawn on a calendar resembled prison bars. Routine was supposed to help, but it hadn't. I counted the days two or three times a night, checking to ensure I didn't miss a day or, even worse, a month wasn't mysteriously added. My mind jumped back and forth to R and R and having to come back after R and R. When I escaped prison, I worried about returning to it.

I tried to focus on the positive. Regrettably, I received word my grandmother had pneumonia. She was too weak to leave the hospital. This was what sacrifice meant. Being here prevented me from saying goodbye. I never even thought to call the hospital. People called us heroes. Soldiering did not feel like heroism. Birthdays, holidays, in-between days, I missed every day, even the saddest days.

To top it off, it snowed. A soldier who was underdressed said, "Hell's freezing over." I couldn't agree more, buddy. Even Mother Nature rebelled at the notion of being there.

On my way back to the TOC after the gym I felt an uncontrollable shiver. A brisk wind on sweaty skin whisked my mind toward simpler times when I was a young scout freezing my ass off nestled in an observation post (OP). I wrote this prose a thousand times in my mind fighting to stay warm. It's titled "Eastern Skies."

Full moons always highlighted feathery clouds. The cloud's wispy tips dangled toward earth meant the upper atmosphere was frigid. When the sun cracked the eastern horizon, I would shiver from anticipation.

I would often contemplate choosing a comfortable desk job so I wouldn't have to be tormented by cold anymore. The idea saddened me because I'd remove myself from outside beauty.

I ached for the warmth of my Bradley. Sunset was the onset of the worst shivering and a constant mental bombardment of fuck the army ensued. The coldest part had always been just before sunrise, so I sat there cussing, sometimes ten hours or more, telling myself to survive another hour. Pick a desk job the next time I reenlist. Just another hour. Minutes after sunrise, I was awestruck. The warmth was refreshing.

That morning walking from the gym toward brigade was the first time I beheld Mesopotamian splendor. I spent hours inside the TOC looking at charts and graphs, preparing for a targeting meeting that ultimately would not matter. If it weren't for school, I would have avoided the building. The war was on autopilot. The battle captain pushed info to us as if the information made a difference to why we were there.

Five thousand soldiers from 1st Cavalry headed home that day. They were coming in from the cold, shivering and shaking, waiting for the sun's radiance to revive them again. They might not comprehend how close they were to eastern skies while they were deployed; ultimately, they would probably miss Iraq's beauty altogether by focusing on her problems.

Most of us would return home shivering from Iraq's shadow. There would not be any relief from the things we had seen while perched in our OP. Being outside the TOC in the cool morning air, watching the sunrise as Iraq's beauty fleeted away, I appreciated the prose I had written.

Another soldier died on Route Senators. This time the IED had been placed in a different spot. Instead of evacuating on Senators, the lieutenant decided to wait for an air MEDEVAC. The soldier lost too much blood. It was a difficult choice.

Should they drive a route exposing themselves to more IEDs, or wait for a bird to arrive? I hated the choice he faced. We were taught indecision was the worst decision. The second part was, don't second-guess the first. Death was a cruel teacher.

Unfortunately, there wasn't a right decision. Damned if you did. Damned if you didn't. The next time, someone else would opt to evacuate on the route in an attempt to avoid his last decision, jeopardizing two soldiers instead of one. The worst part about Iraq was knowing there wasn't a right call.

Spring was almost upon us. I received troubling news that my mother lost her home on Canary Drive. She rented to a friend who defaulted on the obligation. Fourteen acres in Henry County, Georgia, gone because of big-heartedness. Our deployment and living in Germany isolated us when the housing market righted itself. I hated that she struggled to stay afloat.

My grandma was close to going home. Spring didn't feel like a new beginning. I hoped she held on so I could see her one last time. March 6, 2008, marked the halfway point, and on March 3 grandma Lewis passed away. I can't remember if I cried.

The USO sponsored a comedy show. It felt good to laugh. Little things made life bearable. I understood how important Bob Hope was to our troops in Vietnam. I can't recall the comedian or what he said, I just knew it felt good to feel my insides rumble with laughter, if only for a minute.

Noriega was sent to rotate in with Captain Jefferies and me. Noriega went on leave a month later, so we went back to twelve-hour shifts for three weeks. His arrival marked the fifth year in Iraq. President Bush was happy with our progress. He proclaimed the surge had worked. Iraqi politicians were as corrupt as America's. I felt sorry for the next president. He would inherit Bush's bullshit.

Adding salt to wounds, a tornado tore through Atlanta. I tried checking on my dad, but he didn't answer.

Shia Muslims increased their attacks. In one day, we had thirty SIGACTS (significant activities) reported, including indirect fire, an explosively formed penetrator attack (EFPs were designed to cut through tanks), and small arms fire. Fourteen Iraqi police were kidnapped and later released. Not a peep made it into the news cycle. I hoped it wasn't an indication of the coming weeks. Petraeus wasn't looking like the military savior he was made out to be. Iraq resembled Vietnam's smoke and mirrors.

Another 101st soldier was killed by an IED yesterday. Happened in the exact same spot where one went off two days prior. Despite the one we adverted the other day, several erupted within a matter of hours. IEDs were everywhere.

Life and death were in constant flux. It wasn't comparable to being home and watching the news about a car wreck, stabbings, or a nightclub shooting. At home, the news was localized. Here, violence visited every corner.

Whenever an IED hit a convoy, I saw destroyed vehicles being towed through the gate. Our sleeping quarters were near the gate. Sometimes I went to the salvage yard where the damaged vehicles sat. I felt the serrated metal and saw the maroon bloodstains flaking on vehicle floors. I went to contextualize what war was. I needed the details of all the names I collected to voice their opinions.

The smells brought war to life. Burnt blood, black soot, doors unopenable, and jagged metal aided my comprehension of the contact reports. I envisioned having to call in my own contact report as Outlaw Red-Four. Some vehicles were so badly damaged, I wondered how the survivors extricated the incapacitated. The shredded tires and broken axels immobilized my thoughts. This was what an IED on a screen resembled. Cut seat belts, uncollected knee pads, and canteens soldiers had left inside. They would not need these items anymore.

The motor pool was war's end, and the rows upon rows of destroyed vehicles looked like a junkyard of broken dreams. I could finally put my hands around the wreckage and squeeze as I hard as I wanted. I wanted to choke its life! Stop the unrelenting tide of it. War be damned! My forearms were tense and my teeth clenched. I felt foolish and looked around to see if anyone noticed what I had done, releasing my grip from the twisted metal. I was finally made aware without experiencing its fallout. This was as close as I wanted to be to an IED.

I looked destiny in her face every day. If I died today, would my sons know what for? It wouldn't be for oil or freeing the oppressed or for a grandiose scheme. When I was young, I had a gripping feeling of wanting to be remembered. I joined the army to satisfy that feeling. I would always be able to claim I was a soldier.

I finished basic training and began adding credentials to my career. Honor was why these brothers died. They were courageous men and women who should be remembered. I hoped to translate their sacrifice to my sons' lives. I wanted them to live as these soldiers had, balancing on the edge of right and wrong and holding the scale balanced so we could walk from the underside of wickedness to the topside of righteousness.

I prayed my sons would recognize that these soldiers died for something worth living for. They didn't perish for WMDs we would never find. Perhaps, these words would satisfy an innate feeling of wanting my brothers to be more than white marble headstones at Arlington cemetery. I wished for more and wanted a light to be turned back on.

BAQUBAH

"Mankind must put an end to war before war puts an end to mankind." —John F. Kennedy

~May 15, 2008~

Fourth Squadron moved to FOB Warhorse earlier than expected and took over securing the town of Baqubah. Warhorse was larger than Prosperity, but its amenities were lacking. It was almost barbaric. The dirt had dust piles. There weren't many clear days while we were there. Everyone walked around with bandanas covering their mouths to filter the dust. The concrete barriers seemed ten feet higher than at the previous FOBs. The platoons were stretched trying to cover a larger battlespace.

Although our area seemed nonthreatening, it could escalate at any moment. Most of the time, the insurgents went into observation mode before attacking. I envied their patience. They knew we couldn't resist reaching for cheese in their mousetraps. Inshallah (God willing), we'd ignore every trap.

My room was set up and I worked an eight-hour shift which started at midnight. In four months and two weeks, I would be taking R and R leave. Deuce continued getting into trouble. His name would eventually make its way to the installation commander's desk. He had spray-painted a command sergeant major's house with his name. The MPs were able to follow the trail he left to our house. He was caught stealing earrings from the post exchange store. One more infraction and he would be kicked out of Germany.

There wasn't much I could do about it. He pushed me to the point of stillness. Every move I made had an opposite effect. I wished he would find a better path. I could not force him in my direction. God be the final authority—I prayed that prayer often while rubbing the scar on my ankle.

Soldiers began getting careless as the end drew near. The first major accident occurred when a seasoned soldier attempted to clear his .50 caliber machine gun with a bullet which exploded in his hand. He lost part of his finger.

Usually, the unit conducted a safety stand-down. It seemed the command brushed it aside. Another soldier fired a round into a clearing barrel, which was a big no-go. Usually, that kind of mistake carried nonjudicial punishment. This occurrence, leaders ignored it. Not that punishing a soldier was warranted for firing a round into a clearing barrel—after all, that's why it was manufactured. It was the carelessness the accidental discharge represented that alarmed leaders. I felt that whatever luck we had ran thin. I prayed Lieutenant Burks remained our only casualty.

Unluckily, before I left FOB Liberty, I dropped 225 pounds on my chest and suffered a bruised sternum. The spotter wasn't paying attention when my wrist went limp during a bench press. I wasn't aiming for a Purple Heart, but that was my boneheaded moment. It probably beat Krafty nearly blinding himself with a bungee cord.

R and R was a sweet success. I flew Tia and the kids to Atlanta. Total cost of the fun was roughly $10,000. Luckily, combat pay covered it. I made up for all the skipped pool parties. Tia made me appreciate her decision to stay at a bed-and-breakfast. For once, I was glad I wasn't frugal. We binge-watched *24* whenever we weren't trotting to Atlanta's attractions. We spent a week with my family and a week in Alabama for Tia's family reunion.

As hot and sunny as Iraq was, the sun at home felt different. It was muggier but brighter. There were grass and leaves that responded to wind. There was hope and laughter that didn't need comedic timing. R and R blitzed by. By the time I released my first hugs of Tia and the kids, it seemed it was time to hug them goodbye. Of course, my mom and Tia fought back tears when it was time to leave. I hugged my kids extra-tight. Encouraged Deuce to step up and be a man. Everyone knew I wasn't patrolling the streets, but Iraq still represented danger.

Upon my return, I learned a platoon had been ambushed in the palm groves. Two soldiers from Fires Squadron were killed. Plus, a sergeant first class overdosed while huffing paint. They found him in his room. His story even had privates shaking their heads in bewilderment. You never knew what people were dealing with. We saw each other fourteen or more hours a day and still remained clueless about things that mattered. Everyone missed his warning signs. First day back, I was ready to go back on R and R.

I filled out an absentee ballot at work. If I didn't do anything else right, I voted. For whatever reason, I had an overwhelming feeling my vote would prevent others from having to spend fifteen months here. Foolish? Perhaps. But I hoped all the same.

There was a house-borne explosion in Pale Horse's area. Three were wounded. Jeremy Vrooman left for Landstuhl hospital in critical condition. The previous night, the chain of command discussed painting a mural in the hallway for Lieutenant Burks. *If we paint it, we would inevitably paint another,* I thought. I wanted to be wrong. I felt sick for thinking it. Jeremy needed positive energy. Hopefully, there was a surgeon at Landstuhl who had a miracle on standby.

What did you pray when someone was blown into memories? Did you ask for his limbs to be found? For life to continue?

I doubted I could finish my last six years of service. Iraq had taken my purpose. All this loss left me bitter toward a country that didn't seem to care.

So many had died. Would I have the courage to walk across booby-trapped thresholds as they did, and continued doing? House after exploding house, they entered. Would I have their courage if I had to spend another day walking through hell?

October couldn't come quickly enough. We reached a year. We should be leaving; instead, politicians and generals added three additional months. Three months for an extra $1,000 per month to accomplish more. More of what? "WHY WERE WE HERE, PRESIDENT BUSH"?

~July 15, 2008~

Staff Sergeant Jeremy Vrooman succumbed to his injuries. I believe he and Lieutenant Burks were within that deadly thirty-day window.

In a 2011 interview with Fox News, Vrooman's parents said Jeremy didn't have to deploy. He could have stayed on rear detachment, but he wanted to be there for his men. He did not have to enter first. He wanted to be first. If harm was imminent, it would have to hit him to get to his men.

My wife and some other wives went out and partied with him and his wife before he left Germany. He was a sharp-nosed Caucasian married to an ebony beauty. He didn't fit the bill, he was the mint. Tia was hysterical about the news. "I just danced with him," she kept repeating between her gasps for air. "How can this be?" she gasped.

I couldn't provide her an answer. I was silent and just as distraught. The earth lost its ground floor and my legs were in a knee-high fog. It felt like reality had sunk a foot closer toward hell.

Tia said Mrs. Vrooman was inconsolable. The other two soldiers from Fires Squadron who died while I was on R and R were Mixon and Tran. All of 4th Squadron earned Purple Hearts that day. All the tiffs and misunderstandings that happened over that year didn't matter. We were bound by loss.

There's still a wordless void that sits in the pit of my being when I think back to that moment. My pupils tend to widen and I feel like I'm sucked back toward that helpless state. I wish I could describe what that feels like, but I can't. It just feels empty, and the only way it feels halfway better is knowing how unselfish an act Jeremey performed by disregarding the deadliest time and leaving his wife and baby to be with us. He deserves a Medal of Honor, and even that wouldn't be enough to honor his actions.

We came to the home stretch. Reintegration would prove to be the hardest part of the deployment. Being there taught me to let little things go. Focus on big-picture moments. Give more love. Complain less. Play ball. Help with homework. Visit friends. Be there when you say you will.

Home would be an adjustment because my time was somewhat mine. I didn't have to share it with anyone except the TOC. I didn't think I suffered from PTSD, but I knew I was affected by Iraq. I needed to come to terms about the purpose of it. What did we measure our fallen comrade's sacrifice by? We sustained a loss of laughter we'd never know. Whether we championed its cause or not, we had been exposed to America's lie.

The prison-like manner in which I went about counting days had unwittingly made me a prisoner. I have yet to realize the extent to which I was locked into Iraq.

At times, I felt the prayers and support of home. Other times, I felt utterly alone. Through it all, I think God was there. It was the near-misses and what-ifs that tugged hardest. Nothing was certain. Nothing was defined. I listened to heroes who deployed talking about their one or two kills. Sometimes, the number ballooned to three or four. I was glad my number was zero.

Even the soldiers who ransacked and pillaged houses, or belittled Iraqis because they held powerful assault rifles, their souls bore a truth. Everyone who left Iraq held a truth and a lie. What mattered most was the one they chose to reveal.

I prayed the remainder of our unit made it home unscathed. For those who had conquered death and moved on to glory, may they never be forgotten. Whether this war was just or not, history would be the final authority. Whether it was ineffective or effective didn't matter anymore. Only one word mattered: home! I ran to it.

It just so happened that Mat Bocian, who served as my troop XO in Germany, wrote a book of prose. He published a couple of books about his deployments to Iraq. His initial deployment was filled with IEDs and corner-to-corner firefights. Reading his book made me appreciate deploying when I had.

I found it ironic that this piece resonated most. It represents the balance between peace and war and past and present that I felt. He wrote it during his first deployment, but it felt as if I'd encountered the same girl when Outlaw Red cleared those same high-rise buildings. His poem summed up Iraq for me. With his permission, this is "Lorelei," from his book *The Ghosts of Tal'Afar.*

Lorelei
On the 17th floor of the Holland Apartments

One floor from the top, down on Haifa St.
Was a slender but shapely figure with long,
Blonde hair. Three feet or more it seemed.

She stood there in the evenings, in a white tank-top
Faded blue jeans, hair draped over her curves
She did this routinely, as I often saw while
patrolling

So much so that my designated marksmen
Raised their rifles high if only to use their
Scopes to get a better view.

One hot afternoon in the spring we walked
Through the apartments… we stopped to take
five and talk to the residents about power
problems or something like that.

In the group of schoolgirls sitting on a bench
Was our blonde-haired beauty, waiting on the
power so they didn't have to climb seventeen
flights …power being intermittent, you see

Such a lovely girl of 17 or so; with fair olive skin,
And almond-shaped eyes, and her wonderful
hair! We chatted with them for a spell, my 'terp
to relay that when I was 17, we'd take the stairs,
I joked but they insisted it was too many.
Youth…

They were glad we were here, Haifa now safe –

*This girl will be a star someday – a bright star of Iraq.
… she wants to study law,
"Tell her," I say "That she must know – every night on the balcony when she brushes her hair – she; breaks the heart of every Soldier in Baghdad".*

Giggles erupt and our beauty blushes… Then the sun starts to set and the heat dies, lights flicker on. "Well, your elevator is here, and we have to go." … the elevator doors open, and our beauty limps in, that shapely right leg on her gorgeous hips near useless; she hobbles inside.

My heart sank. 'Too many stairs,' I thought. Dammit.

A neighbor saw me wave and told me her story; Suicide car-bomb. On her way to school. Innocent bystander. A victim. Shattered hip, busted leg – no one will marry her, not if she can't have kids…

The wave of emotion hit me… I could've cried right then and there, a lump in my throat.

All of my hope died there that day.

I never had hope for Iraq ever again.

By Matthew Bocian (thanks, XO, for lending your truth).

Hindsight being our better vision, I hoped that Lorelei's neighbor was wrong and she became a star in Iraq.

Hopefully, Iraq would evolve into the sparks of beauty I witnessed. Hopefully, we carried as much of her beauty as we did her pain. Lorelei represented Iraq: beautiful yet broken. A place where hope gave way to hate. A place where only questions remained.

~September 18, 2008~

I was scheduled to leave on advanced party in a few days. Kuwait to out-process, then Germany by October 2. It was time to start packing and place this journal in safekeeping. I should be grateful for the experience. Applying what I learned would be key moving forward. I survived the "process." At least, I hoped.

My last entry from Iraq, the tarmac was sultry as it had been fourteen months before. Now, I was perched on a cot inside a tent to avoid the sun's power. I scribbled a quick letter to myself before stuffing the journal into a duffel bag, wishing that my time in Iraq be completely lobotomized from memory.

Dear Me,

Where was joy and why did we hate? Objects out of order. Mad about unemptied trash. Questions unanswered, and we never raised a hand. Failed grades while daydreaming; banished to timeout. Debt, or freedom thereof. Nightclubs. Drinking. Rutted ways of thinking. Schools. Degrees. Promotions and permanent change of stations. No longer dreaming in color. Family events. The dirty uncle nieces avoided. Facing us, without the implications of them. Cussing and fussing. Laughter and pain. How had hate maintained so much energy? Were words tools of destruction? Could a kind word really change our world or have we blotted out the sun by building higher walls? Take it from me, walls trapped us in. Kids and respect. Pants sagged. Belts clung to kneecaps. Was mine really yours? Or could we be divided by divorce decree? Laws were skewed. Innocence abused. Frustrated. Uncommunicated. Were we viewing the world from end to end or just from our point in time? Did we chisel away the concrete whenever we felt boxed in? We were never as high as we thought, nor as low as we believed. We were always where God had wanted us. Yes, some decisions led us further from truth, but it was never as far it seemed.

Why I kept a journal was of no concern. I just wanted my voice to be heard. Not with turmoil or strife, but with peace and might. Only a foolish man would remain silent when everything within him screamed.

A wise man would order his words and discover the truths that lay between. Sometimes, the best teacher recognized, he or she would always be a student. There would never come a time when I would not ask why. The journal closed, reintegrating to home life would be the most precarious part of the journey.

During our last week in Kuwait before returning to Germany, soldiers and spouses took classes on what was to be expected. Soldiers headed back to a family unit that had adjusted to them being gone. We were coming home with a great deal of ugliness on our minds. At some point, friction would detonate.

REINTEGRATION

"Home is where the heart's tears can dry at their own pace." — Vernon Baker

It was weird reliving those experiences. The first couple of pages brought back feelings and images I'd kept hidden. When I returned to Germany, there was a major adjustment period. Tia and I fought a lot. I was drinking to the point that my character turned unrecognizable. Sleep was a leprechaun hiding his treasure. I remained tense and acted as if I were still on patrol, scanning for possible threats.

Most veterans had a hard time adjusting, including the Fobbits. All the signs were there: irritable, angry, startled easily, vigilant, and paranoid—telltale signs something wasn't right. Most paid it no attention. The army programmed us to function on four hours of sleep or less. Anger was a byproduct of submitting our souls to the business of sending jihadists to their creator. Even if we never pulled a trigger, we were prepared to. I limped along with my aches and pains for eight more years after Iraq.

I left Germany and became a Reserve Officers' Training Corps (ROTC) instructor and applied my experience to helping cadets commission as officers. This was my favorite quote for them: "A student said to his master, 'You teach me fighting, but you talk about peace. How do you reconcile the two?' The master replied, 'It is better to be a warrior in a garden than to be a gardener in a war.'"

After ROTC, in June 2013, I went to Camp Casey, Korea where my story took its sharpest turn. It was where I noticed that the realities of the war had left their residue.

While stationed in Korea, I had the opportunity to travel to Cebu, Philippines. I took the trip alone on Labor Day weekend. Every paradise seemed to hide the disenfranchised behind the palm trees. This place was no different. Beautiful beaches were riddled with mid-size crabs and Jet Skis skipped across shallow waves underneath the parasailers. This side of the Pacific flourished with seaweed and starfish easing across rocks and pier supports. The nightlife offered anything and everything. The entire island vied for my economic attention.

As I walked the streets outside the resort, there was a familiarity. It was as if poverty unleashed semen and birthed an economic depression. The men and women suffered from one and a half children too many. If that half child was erased from the statistical tally, the poor might be elevated to the bottom level of middle class. Their desire to survive was monopolized by our willingness to capitalize on survival instincts. The world was afflicted by that need-versus-greed dynamic.

As I continued walking on a dirt road, a goat grazed on a single patch of grass. Barefoot kids played tag. Scooters blitzed past like overstuffed dragonflies. Although I felt safe, if I blinked the scene might become eerily similar to Baghdad. *How far was al-Qaeda's reach?* I wondered. I was reintroduced to worldly despair. I attempted to be less conspicuous, but I stood six inches taller than the tallest person. An underlying fear sprang forth. It was unseen and undocumented. I was haunted from being hunted and wanted to sink low to avoid possible sniper fire.

The first night was exciting, drinking local rum. I hung out at the beach until the tide shifted and the ocean returned to land. While I was perched in a hammock writing, something sinister occurred near a naval base in Manila.

Whenever I was away from Tia for extended periods of time, I would drift back to memories of our beach excursion. The moon was so bright that it blocked the stars. I wrote:

Rescued.

Did you enjoy the ocean as much as the ocean enjoyed you? Were you able to find your ebb and flow? Did seaweed get tangled in your toes? Heard you had bathed in rain. Did your sensuous scent drip upon a blanket of sand? Did you follow the Lord's footsteps slowly, the way time intended, or did you run as if wind was chasing you? Did you explore the depths or wade right at shore's edge? Or lay there at night and let the moon fall between your thighs? Were you impregnated by the sounds of waves crashing on you? Did you come in warm waters that beckoned or did an ocean form within you? Who was the captain that floated above you? When you lay there, did you dare move? Did his ship wreck when he fell victim? Were you left stranded on an island? Was your SOS one of distress or a sign saying, "Leave me alone for an hour or two, then after that, we can do what it do?"

Were you rescued? Swept away by the scent of your own perfume? Oceans and thoughts of you. Were you rescued?

The following morning, I awakened with a throbbing headache and thirsting for water. It was almost 1100 hours by the time I was greeted by a hotel employee. My unit called and said U.S. personnel were recalled.

Apparently, a maid discovered an attractive young woman strangled in a marine's hotel room near Manila, which sparked an international incident. The accused had been drinking and solicited the young lady's company. He brought her back to his room where he discovered that she was a he. The maid found the victim with her head submerged in a toilet.

In an instant, the marine became the newest installment of *Snapped*. I did not want to tarnish other veterans who suffered from PTSD by saying he had it. Truthfully, I did not think he had ever deployed. Was it a far stretch to conclude his combat training played a role? Was it repressed sexuality? Whatever it was, it was human debauchery. And for me, it represented how the military placed us in irrevocable circumstances. The rage and callousness he exhibited was manifested in me at the beginning of 2018.

I was two years into my stroke recovery sitting upstairs in a recliner drinking heavily in the home where I now reside. Depression, debilitating back pain—I didn't rightly know where my head was. I think I was waiting for the stroke to return and finish the job. Tia walked by the door and said something casually. I did not hear what she said, but I felt attacked and shouted, "So what!"

Puzzled, Tia walked away, then came back a few minutes later wanting to know what was bothering me. I rushed at her and slammed the door, yelling "Leave me the fuck alone!"

The entire house reverberated as she stumbled backwards. For the next few hours she was tormented with fear. She later said my eyes looked demonic when I charged at her.

I would not find out until later that the simplest things may cause a PTSD sufferer to go from mild-mannered to hostile. Liquor and beer as a chaser didn't help.

Immediately after nearly unhinging the door, I slumped into my recliner, looked at my palms, and asked, *What the hell just happened?*

My counselor said combat veterans' psyches were constantly exposed to fight-or-flight while deployed, and when we return home it doesn't shut off. The simplest thing could trigger disaster.

As a scout, everything had to be done in a certain order or people could die. When we returned to the civilian sector, many veterans struggled to recalibrate. Life rarely operated within life-or-death parameters. So what if the car didn't get filled when it was at a quarter-tank. So what? So what? So what? Granted, the marine's case was not mine, but mine had almost ended tragically.

Tia was so afraid she went to her friend's house to let me cool off. When she returned home, she slept downstairs with her pistol. Our youngest son came downstairs for a drink. She feared I was coming to finish the deed. She stood hastily, pointed the gun toward the threat, then lowered it, her hands trembling and thumb fumbling with the safety lever. I nearly caused my own worst tragedy. A few days later, I sought more mental help and refrained from drinking liquor.

No one deserved having to house those kinds of demons. Our spouses deserved better. Most veterans didn't realize a darkness festered. By the time it surfaced, its tendrils had a tight grip on our psyche.

At Fort Bliss, I had been in outpatient counseling with James Fleming, a soldier who was in the process of medically retiring. He was sent to Iraq several times and committed suicide shortly after he was discharged from service. He could no longer fight his demons. His zippered volcano could no longer hold all the heat and torment he held inside.

The same haunting stare I saw when I was in Iraq listening to my buddies retell their stories, James had it. Every day, he came to our sessions and fell deeper into his chasm. The devil was undressing his pain before or eyes and James rarely, if ever, spoke. He was a beautiful person who was colored by war's ugliness.

A soldier from Outlaw Red calls me every now and then. He suffers from PTSD and depression. I encourage him as best I can, but I fear there's a stranglehold on him as well. Every time he calls, I can tell he is being pulled further and further away. And I'm helpless trying to pull him to my broken plateau.

For too long, I viewed this issue through an uneducated perspective. Basing whether I had PTSD on soldiers who had experienced the worst war had to offer. Truth was, it only took one day in Iraq for its dark seed to sprout.

Hopefully, my story will help other veterans or spouses seek help. I lost a lot since the story first began. I gave more than I intended when I first joined the army. But through God's grace, luck, or some divine universal order, I am still here. Still struggling with the lie of it all. Lies that began unravelling when I had my stroke.

The truth was, I was tired of living and tired of asking why. Everything would be easier in an hour or two. Close your eyes. Let life fade away. *Don't be nobody's hero.*

During counseling, I learned I needed to come to terms with why we had to go to Iraq. I wrestled with this question before, during, and after. The answer didn't come until recently.

Sergeant First Class Pope came to Fort Benning for training. Since I retired there, we linked up. We reminisced as old soldiers did. I asked him why we had to go to Iraq.

"You know, Sergeant Lewis, I ask myself that a lot. I think we went to remind ourselves America ain't so bad. We can sleep and not worry about somebody coming and snatching us from our homes. Bullets aren't whizzing by as we stand here in this parking lot shooting the shit. We have running water. Our trash gets collected. I know over there, there were kids barely scraping by and parents just trying to protect their families," he replied.

With the journal properly shelved and my résumé for sanitation engineer readied for submission, it was odd peering back. Maybe it was that simple. We needed Iraq in order to see life in a different light.

When it's dark, and a match is struck, its flame is seen miles away. Maybe we had to go through it to adjust our eyes to simpler moments. Darkness intensifies the dimmest light. We didn't require bright lighthouses to make it back to shore. Our eyes adjusted to darkness well. Maybe, all we needed was for someone to strike up a conversation to spark a light we thought had been forever extinguished.

Maybe Iraq was a reminder of how bad life could be. A reminder of a promise I made when I first arrived in Iraq—to live a more appreciative life. I forgot that promise when I lay down beside my bed in Fort Bliss wanting to die. Not even willing to be a hero unto myself. What a shame it would have been to give in when all the soldiers I cherished would have never laid down and died.

They charged into houses. They looked fear in the face and yelled, "Bring it on bastard!" They were the heroes my mother-in-law prayed I did not become. I almost lived up to her words too well.

Now that I can look at the question in its entirety, Western foreign policy went awry long before Truman's doctrine, the events of September 11, and the bloodshed afterwards. I can see the total price paid and the taxation that still rests heavy on our hearts. Now, I understand why the author of Deuteronomy 32:35 wrote: "Vengeance is mine, thus sayeth the Lord." The question was never for us, but about us. The answer resides in our ability to so quickly throw away the sacred for the corruptible.

Now that we are eighteen years into fighting and certain cities have established special veterans' courts to deal with our unique cases, accounting for lives lost, the technological enhancements in prosthetics, advancements in the weaponry and security industries, and our insatiable need to tap oil reserves dry, I wonder if there will ever come a time when we have what we need? Why wasn't six months enough, versus eighteen years and counting?

Maybe, Iraq was meant for America to fight for peace more violently so our sons and daughters would not have to. Maybe, the war was so I could hold my wife tighter than before. Maybe, Iraq was meant for me to meet some of the bravest souls I have ever known, and to honor them through living.

I held on to this foolish notion: somehow their sacrifice would serve as a reminder why it was better to not have to ask why at all. Their sacrifice continues to be the reason I ask. War has yet to become so pointless and grotesque a thing that it has made us want to love more and hate less. That's the scariest thing of all, and only God knows why.

Sadly, I took too long fulfilling my dream. My eldest son passed away before I could make him proud of me. He and two of his beloved friends died in a tragic car accident July 28, 2018.

He became the man I had hoped he would. Despite my efforts to keep him tied to mediocre paths, he produced several astonishing rap songs on SoundCloud under the name Deuce 808. No matter what he faced, he excelled at producing music. I'll strive to live a better why for him and the other heroes more courageous than I. Rest amongst the stars, son.

They say tomorrow isn't promised. I know it is. Somewhere out there, I know my words ring true. Farewell rarely lasts forever. Goodbye doesn't extend beyond time. The end could very well be the best way to start our finest chapter if we let it.

Come out of the cold my friends. We need our heroes home.

Deuce and I, Mount Rainier, Washington

ABOUT THE AUTHOR

Lewis served twenty-two years, two months, and twelve days in the U.S. Army as a calvary scout. He lives near Fort Benning, Georgia, with his lovely wife, Tia. This is his first publication. He has earned several different degrees: an associate's degree in general studies, a bachelor's in business administration, and a master's certificate in creative writing, which, aside from a few culinary school classes, was his most enjoyable. Besides taking on the role of author, watching his niece, nephews, and two grandchildren snag a bluegill or two is how he likes spending his time. He has a passion for writing and is working toward publishing more prose and short stories.

ts.lewis.publishing@outlook.com

Made in the
USA
Lexington, KY